As The Rock Flower Blooms

Rosemary A. Watson

Overseas Missionary
Fellowship
1058 Avenue Road
Toronto, Ontario M5N 2C6

AN OMF BOOK

ISBN 9971-972-17-4

First published 1984

OMF BOOKS are distributed by
OMF, 404 South Church Street,
Robesonia, Pa. 19551, USA and
by OMF, Belmont, The Vine,
Sevenoaks, Kent, TN13 3TZ,
UK and other OMF offices.

Published by Overseas Missionary Fellowship (IHQ)
Ltd., 2 Cluny Road, Singapore 1025, Republic of
Singapore, and printed by Singapore National Printers
(Pte) Ltd.

Contents

Acknowledgments

I AM DEEPLY indebted to the many missionaries who have shared with me their memories of this stalwart Christian tribesman. John and Dorothy Davis, Ron and Kathy Smith, Ellie Hoffmeister, David Fewster, and many others have been very helpful in providing details of events that happened after I left Laos in 1964.

Although like myself some of these friends are no longer members of the OMF, we still feel like one family. In spirit we continue to labor through our prayers and gifts alongside that great mission founded by J. Hudson Taylor in 1865 – the China Inland Mission, now called the Overseas Missionary Fellowship.

Many grateful thanks are also due to Armand Heiniger and Hermann Christen for their advice and for the inspiration and example of their lives. It has been a privilege to work with the missionaries of Mission Evangélique, which invited the OMF to join hands in taking the Gospel to Laos.

I especially thank God for my husband Lindell, for without his patience and encouragement during the past few years I would never have been able to complete this book.

Preface

IN THE SPRING of 1961 we missionaries heard that in another area of Laos the son of a *shaman* (spirit priest or witchdoctor) had trusted in Jesus. Immediately we began to pray that he would stand firm, because in a country like Laos, bound by superstition, Buddhism, and demon worship, following the true God is always a lonely business. Many there have professed faith in Christ only to turn back to paganism when trials came. We sometimes called this young tribal man "Mr. Stand", partly because of his name and partly because we believed God would enable him to stand true to Christ.

It had taken my fellow missionaries several years of labor and prayer to penetrate this tribe with the Gospel. The people deliberately isolated themselves and resisted any form of change. But God has ways of breaking down even the most fiercely guarded fortress.

A tradition had sprung up among earlier generations in this tribe that when the lichen on the rocks began to bloom, it would be a sign that the unknown Good Spirit was at last going to reveal Himself and send deliverance from the powers of evil.

Lichen does not normally bear flowers, nor do hearts depraved by sin and demon worship reach out toward God. But anything can happen when Christians have covered an area with intercessory prayer and God begins to move.

Several other missionary women and I had the great privilege of teaching this young Christian during the first year of his walk with Jesus. He left an indelible mark upon my heart and life, and for years I have longed for this opportunity to share his story with the world. Many other missionaries also influenced his life, so this is not a story of anything I accomplished, but only a report of what God did for a humble tribesman who dared to stand alone and trust Jesus when everything seemed against him.

The Christians mentioned in this book did not have the multitude of spiritual helps that we possess: abundant Christian literature, great Bible teachers and evangelists, and modern communication aids to help spread the Gospel. Yet they accomplished a great deal by their simple faith and obedience to Christ. The same God who transformed this illiterate tribal boy into a great leader can also touch and transform your life and personality, however inadequate you may feel in yourself.

As you read these pages I trust you will not simply admire this courageous Christian, but will also feel called to become a prayer partner to uphold him and the many other believers who have remained faithful to Christ during the years since missionaries left Laos. The names of many people and places have been changed to protect the Christians, but God knows their real names and delights to meet their physical, material and spiritual needs as you and I intercede for them. You can obtain regular prayer fuel by writing to Mekong Prayer Fellowship at your local OMF office.

When all the tribes and nations are gathered before God's throne and the rewards are handed out, certain prayer warriors from across the earth will be recognized as having had a tremendous influence on the life and ministry of this humble tribesman, although they never met him in the flesh. What a great meeting that will be when all suffering and trials are over and these intercessors at last look into his eyes and grasp his hands! Will you be one of them?

May all glory and praise be given to Jesus our Redeemer, who made all these things possible through His power and grace!

Rosemary A. Watson.

1

A Seed of Doubt

A SMALL GROUP of men plodded wearily down a steep mountain trail through tangled forest. Some were barefoot and wore only loincloths, but others were dressed in tattered shirts, black shorts and sandals made from old truck tires. Each one carried on his back a large bamboo basket filled with short logs of pitch pine.

They were tired now, although they had had a delightful time chopping wood in the cool mountain air, so much more pleasant than the hot, humid plains where they lived. They always enjoyed these expeditions, although in recent years some danger was involved. Not only was there the possibility of capture by rebel soldiers hiding in the forest, but they could be fined by the government. Pitch pine trees were becoming scarce, and the authorities had forbidden them to cut down any more of the trees. But the Taway people had always used pine chips to illuminate their homes in the evenings, and these mountains were the only place they knew where this special kind of pitch pine grew. They had stripped each log of the outer bark and wood and were taking home only the pitchy heart of the trees, which would ignite easily and burn slowly. Later they would return to gather the bark and wood chips for fuel.

Silently they scrambled down the rocky trail, often grabbing a tree or vine to steady themselves as their loads swayed precariously. Finally their gray-haired leader paused under a large tree where the path widened.

"Let's stop here and rest a bit," he said. "Peng, take my load." A short, muscular young man lifted the bamboo basket and set it on the ground, then turned and waited for his own load to be removed. He had a rather square head, and his hair cropped very short on the sides but left longer on top made his face seem narrow and serious even when relaxed. After taking Peng's basket from his shoulders Loong squatted in the shade and took out his pipe. Peng smiled at his uncle and settled next to him with a contented sigh.

"It feels good to sit down," he said.

As the others found comfortable positions nearby, two young men remained standing, looking down at their companions disapprovingly.

"It'll take us another hour to get to the village," Heng said, shifting his load impatiently.

"You've been complaining all day," Peng said. "Relax! We're not in danger. We haven't seen any evidence that the rebel soldiers have been up here recently." He was tired and felt cross, but he forced himself to smile as he motioned to Heng to sit beside him. But his friend stubbornly remained standing.

"I'm not thinking of the rebels," Heng retorted sharply. "I just want to get home." He shivered slightly and drew closer to the shelter of a large boulder to escape the breeze. The ragged shirt he wore didn't give his thin body much warmth. It was quite cool at this time of the year when the sun went down, especially two thousand feet above the plains.

"We'd better keep our voices down," warned a large man wearing only a loincloth. "Enemy soldiers could be hiding in the forest; you know they often make their own paths. Remember how they captured my son last summer even though our guards were watching the trails." His companions grunted sympathetically.

"I remember that night well," Heng said, his dark eyes flashing angrily. "My cousin was captured, too. Some of our people have been acting like cowards ever since. If more men had come with us today we wouldn't be so late getting home."

"Some people are lazy as well as fearful," commented Heng's companion. "My brother will soon run out of pine chips and he'll ask for some of mine to make light in his house. I should just let him sit in darkness. Why should I risk my life while he stays home in safety?"

"Our people have always helped one another," Loong declared. "You young people think only of yourselves."

"Some men had to stay to guard the village," Peng added quietly. "Women and children cannot protect themselves." He felt his temper rising but struggled to control it, and rubbed the top of his head in agitation.

"Your brother isn't much help." Heng glared down at him. "Why does Khap always have an excuse to go somewhere when we need him?"

Peng's long brown face reddened with embarrassment and he sprang to his feet, his fists clenched angrily and his square jaw firmly set. He didn't always understand his brother's actions, but he was determined to defend him. "Khap is brave and ready to fight any time, and so am I," he retorted. "Today he went to visit a friend who has been to the city. He'll bring us news of the war when he comes home."

"Maybe he takes secret messages to the enemy," Heng suggested bitterly. "Or does he just like to have a good time with the village girls?"

Peng's mouth dropped open and he stared at Heng in astonishment. Angry words flooded his mind, and he felt like pushing Heng over the steep edge of the trail. He struggled to regain a cool heart, for only a crude person would let his emotions boil over. What was wrong with Heng?

Before he could answer, his uncle Loong rose to his feet. "Let's not argue," he said firmly. "It's time to go."

The men took up their loads and filed down the rocky path, but Peng hung back, feeling worried. What was wrong with his friend? They had played together for years. He remembered the time they had tied a squirrel's tail on a long pole and pushed it through a crack in the bamboo wall of a house, frightening the spirit priests who were having a séance inside! He had had such fun with Heng. What had changed him?

Slowly following his companions, Peng was barely aware of the monkeys chattering in the shadowed woodland and the cicadas buzzing in the trees. He wondered why his brother went away so often. Khap never seemed content; he was restless and ambitious, determined to have his own way. If he didn't settle down soon, he would surely get into trouble. On the other hand, Peng admired his brother's adventurous spirit. He enjoyed his company, and they often talked late into the night, even though they sometimes disagreed.

At last the trail emerged from the gloomy forest. Peng stopped briefly to look out over the dry terraced rice fields below him. Far in the distance he could see the faint gleam of the Say River threading its way across the plains. Although quite wide where it curved around the town of Mong in the distance, this river was said to be small compared to the mighty Mekong River which spanned the length of Laos from China to Cambodia like a royal road. Peng had never seen the Mekong, for it passed on the other side of the mountains before flowing on south across Cambodia and Vietnam into the sea.

Ban[1] Dao, his home village, was directly below him, hidden among thick clumps of papaya and

---

[1]*Ban* means *village* in Laotian.

mango trees interspersed with tall graceful coconut palms. The scent of wood smoke drifted upward from the homes where supper was cooking. He could hear water gurgling in a covered cistern nearby, and through the under-brush he glimpsed the sections of hollowed-out bamboo which carried the clear spring water down to the village. His heart leaped with joy and contentment. He was very proud of the cleverness of his tribe. He never wanted to live anywhere except among the Taway people.

Although his tribe was small, less than five thousand persons living in their few villages at the foot of the mountains, they were vigorous and independent in nature. Most tribes in Laos had been pushed up into the hills by the lowland Laotians, but the Taway still lived on the edge of the plains, growing rice in the same terraced fields their forefathers had cultivated for gene-rations.

The path leveled off suddenly and led through a grove of huge trees where the ground was ablaze with a carpet of red and yellow leaves which had fallen during the dry season. The leaves crackled under his sandals as he hurried to catch up with his companions. He glimpsed the men in the distance just before the path again dropped steeply and wound between two large rocks. The remains of an ancient avalanche stretched below him, the village houses scattered haphazardly among huge boulders. According to tribal traditions, these had fallen from the mountain many years before his ancestors settled here. Everyone believed that very strong spirits lived in the stones.

Dusk had fallen when he entered the village. In front of each house there was a fetish made of chicken feathers hung on small bamboo ornaments stuck into the ground, indicating the homes were dedicated to the spirits. The invisible world was very real to Peng and his tribe. They believed they couldn't survive without the protection of the beings which indwelt the trees, rocks and fields about them.

Peng glanced up at a neighbour's house which towered above him, built on stilts twice his height. He shivered as he noticed a bundle of fresh leaves dangling from the porch, showing the house was *kalaam*.[2] Someone in the family must have died that day! Now it was forbidden to enter the home until the spirits were appeased and the leaves were removed. Many people, including several children, had died from a mysterious illness during the past week, and tomorrow a feast would be held to placate the spirits that had brought the sickness. The ancestor spirits were easily offended, and it was difficult to please them. His own father was a *shaman* who told the people what offerings to make. Still, Peng's heart chilled with fear whenever he thought of the evil spirits. If only there were some way to escape their control!

---

[2]taboo

As he hurried on through the village in the fading light he looked eagerly at the house where Lansee lived. He knew she was probably inside eating with her parents, so he restrained himself from calling out to her. He thought Lansee was the most beautiful girl in Ban Dao. Remembering that he would see her tomorrow at the feast, he smiled to himself and his step quickened. Even though he hated being in bondage to the spirits, he still enjoyed the feasts, the fun and music. And since he was the eldest son in his family, soon he would become a spirit priest like his father. Then he would know how to appease the spirits by blood sacrifices and secret magic spells. Unconsciously he drew his shoulders back and walked with a firmer step, his back straight and his chin lifted proudly.

Then he heard a shout and saw his brother climbing the path toward him. Khap had returned safely! "What's the news?" he called.

"Lang finally arrived home this morning," Khap answered, puffing from the steep climb. "The truck he was riding was delayed because several bridges had been blown up by the rebels. They robbed the driver and all the passengers, but they finally let Lang come on through after temporary bridges had been made."

Peng sighed. "There's trouble on every side for our people. Many are dying of fever and now the war comes closer. What have we done to make the spirits so angry?"

"That's what I want to talk to you about. Let's

sit here for a few minutes," Khap said, motioning to a wide flat rock beside the path. Peng sat down beside his brother, gingerly adjusting the heavy load of logs on his back.

"Maybe our troubles don't come from the spirit world," Khap suggested. His round, pleasant face was suddenly serious as he watched for his brother's reaction.

"Oi!" Peng was startled to hear Khap voice such a radical thought. "What do you mean?"

"I'm tired of living in bondage to the spirits. Lang says I could easily get a job working for the Lao Publique in Solane," Khap announced. "Maybe there I'll find answers for the troubles that plague us."

Peng's mouth dropped open and he stared at his brother. "If you're hired by the public works department you'll have to repair roads and dig holes. You know it's *kalaam* for anyone in our tribe to dig a hole in a place where none have existed before! The spirits will punish you!"

"I'll stay far away where they can't reach me," Khap said confidently. "I want to earn money and become rich. I hear there are some foreigners in the city, and I'd like to see how they live."

Peng marveled at his brother's ambition. "You'll do well, for you're very clever," he said. "You might even have learned French someday if our school hadn't burned down." He sighed as he recalled the devious methods the village leaders had used to prevent the Taway people from learning the ways of the Laotians. Then he warned, "Father will be unhappy if you leave home."

"He'll let me go. He wants me to have heart-rest," Khap declared. "But don't tell him I'll be digging holes."

Peng nodded. Their father was kind and generous, not like some of the other village spirit priests, but still he would be upset that Khap was not loyal to their tribal traditions.

"Let me carry the wood the rest of the way," Khap offered as his brother struggled to his feet.

"No," Peng said, shaking his head, "It's not far to the house."

Khap helped him balance his heavy load, and they hurried through the village. In the deepening darkness they could see their neighbors preparing for the night, chasing their pigs and chickens into pens, or just relaxing on their high porches. Several friends shouted greetings, and some exchanged jokes with Khap as they hastened along the path toward their home.

Peng glanced up admiringly at his tall younger brother. People respect Khap, regardless of what Heng says, he thought. Khap is always moving ahead, trying something new, whereas I seem to stand still. But someday I'll be a leader of my people, a *shaman* who can deliver them from the power of the demons . . . although of course no one can be completely free from the demons. He recalled Khap's words, and a seed of doubt sprouted in his mind. He frowned in perplexity, wondering, could it be possible that our troubles don't come from the evil spirits after all?

2

The Threat

WHEN THEY REACHED home their small brown dog barked its welcome and came for a pat on the head. Khap gripped the heavy basket so Peng could slip his arms out of the rough straps of vine. Setting the basket on the ground, Khap then helped his brother pile the short pitchy logs neatly near the chicken coop under the house. The full moon hovered above the trees, giving them just enough light in the darkness. Agile as monkeys, they quickly climbed to the porch, their strong toes gripping the prongs of broken-off branches which served as rungs on the rustic bamboo ladder. Neither missed a step even though the long pole swayed and rotated under their weight.

Khap sniffed the air hungrily. "I think we're having fish *keng*[1] for supper."

Peng nodded. "Ying must have had a good catch at the river today." He took a long drink of water from the gourd hanging beside the doorway, then offered it to Khap. They ducked their heads and entered the low doorway. Nodding a greeting to their father Samat who

---

[1] A *keng* is similar to a stew or soup, with small pieces of meat and vegetables cooked in a thin broth.

was already eating, they seated themselves on the bamboo mat near a steaming pot of stew.

Peng took a spoon and a brightly colored enamel plate from beside the fire pit. Helping himself to boiled rice, he spooned some of the fish stew on top. Khap also dished up a large serving, and they ate eagerly. The thin broth of the *keng* contained only a few tiny fish and fresh water shrimp flavored with chopped green onions, hot peppers and lemon grass. Like the others, Peng hadn't eaten since early morning, but the simple meal quickly filled the void in his stomach.

"This *keng* is delicious!" he called to his mother who was eating at the back of the room with his twelve-year-old sister Ying. Suk smiled but made no reply. Taway women were expected to remain quietly in the background during mealtime.

The dim interior of the house held no furniture and was quite bare except for the clay firebed in the center. On the wooden floor near one wall lay a few clay pots, a machete, and big brass gong which had been in the family for generations. A crossbow hung from the rafters above. At the back of the large room a small section was partitioned off by a woven bamboo wall; this was the sleeping area used by Samat and his wife. Everyone else slept on mats placed along the walls of the main room; on cold nights these were moved near the fire for comfort. A narrow window shutter under the low thatched eaves was propped open by a short piece of bamboo, letting in an occasional gust of fresh air. The soot accumulated on the blackened rafters gave the room a musty smell which mingled pleasantly with the smoke of the fire now fading on the raised bed of ashes.

"Ying has learned to use the fish traps well," Khap said as he helped himself to more stew and rice. "We haven't had meat or fish for a long time."

"There will be plenty of meat at the feast tomorrow," Samat said. He smiled at his sons, revealing broken teeth blackened from many years of chewing betel nut. Yet the smile transformed his narrow, serious face and brought sunshine into the room. Although he had many burdens he was a cheerful, loving man.

"And much rice wine," Peng added with a sheepish grin, looking down quickly as if he had said too much. He didn't want to mention Lansee yet. She was special, not like other girls he had known.

Khap made no comment. He was wondering how long it would take to walk over the mountains to Solane. He longed to tell his father about his plans but knew this was not the right time to admit his doubts about serving the spirits. If the sickness spread he might be blamed. After the feast was over, he would tell his father and leave. For many months he had been secretly planning this trip, and now at last the rice harvest was nearly completed and the family could easily finish without him.

Samat wiped his mouth with the back of his hand and lifted the gourd dipper from a bucket of water at his side. He took a long drink, then rinsed the dipper by swirling the remaining water round its edges, finally flicking the last drops towards a dark corner of the house. As he went out on the porch he felt anxious and tense. He sensed something was bothering Khap but decided to wait until he was ready to discuss it. Usually Khap was wild with anticipation before a feast day, but this time it seemed to be Peng who was more excited.

Soon Peng came outside and squatted beside his father. Samat put some grated dried betel nut and lime paste on a small leaf and rolled it into a tiny package. Popping it into his mouth, he chewed it noisily with obvious enjoyment. Every few minutes he leaned over the edge of the verandah and spat out a stream of bright red juice. Peng thought this was an ugly habit, but he said nothing. People claimed that betel nut relieved toothaches and calmed their nerves, and he supposed nearly everyone had an addiction of some kind. Neither he nor his father liked to smoke, although most Taway grew tobacco and rolled their own cigarettes or smoked a pipe.

Quietly father and son discussed the harvest. It was small this year because of the drought, but Peng knew there was still plenty of rice to eat. His family had several storehouses; one granary contained rice harvested two years ago. Although the river was very low, sufficient water still trickled down from the spring up on the mountain, so they had everything they needed.

At last Peng and his father went inside and lay on their mats. Everyone else was asleep, tired from the day's work. The village was quiet except for an occasional dog barking at the moon. Wrapped in the soft blanket of darkness, the peaceful village slept.

★   ★   ★   ★

Peng awoke early the next morning to the usual sound of the village women pounding rice for the day's meals. *Thump, thump, thump*! He rolled over and tried to go back to sleep, but he was too excited. He would see Lansee today!

Finally he got up and went outside, moving carefully so as not to shake the plank floor and wake his brother and sister. Khap lay nearby, wrapped in a thin army blanket. Ying slept on the other side of the room under a heavier blanket bought in town. Peng knew his father had already left to present the offerings to the spirits.

From the verandah Peng looked down on his mother pounding the husks off the rice. She gripped a thick pole with both hands and time after time brought it down forcefully on the rice piled in a hollowed-out tree stump, occasionally pausing to catch her breath.

All over the village the women were laboring at their early morning chore with a jagged rhythm. *Thump, THUMP, thump, thump*! The familiar sound made Peng's heart feel warm although the morning air was cool. He had slept in the shorts he wore yesterday, and his bare shoulders felt chilled.

After Khap woke up he would find a clean shirt to put on for the feast. He stood and stretched, attempting to warm himself. He enjoyed the cold season. In a few months the monsoon rains would begin, and then there would be no relief from the oppressive heat and humidity.

Squatting down again and looking over the village, Peng thought of the two men and six children who had recently died with fever. Where were they now? Did their souls hover over the village demanding appeasement, as the spirit priests claimed? He shivered at the thought of death. Perhaps the sacrifice offered today would satisfy the spirits. He resolved he would have a good time at the feast and try to forget his fears.

By noontime a large crowd had gathered in the center of the village near the headman's house. Peng and Khap joined a group of young men beside a low bamboo platform where food had been set out on banana leaves. The pig sacrificed early that morning had been roasted and was now ready to eat. Peng joined in the good-natured laughter and smiled at Heng, but received only a menacing glare in return.

At last a group of girls arrived with Lansee in their midst. Immediately the young men surrounded them, each hoping to find a partner for the day. The girls wore short skirts made of a heavy red and black striped cotton fabric woven by the Huay tribe. Taway women traded rice and other commodities for this colorful material, which they much admired. Worn low on the hips, the skirts reached only to the mid-thigh and were just a flat piece of cloth wrapped around the waist. Some of the girls, Lansee included, also had on a sleeveless slip-on blouse made of the same dark material. The others wore only a bra, but all were considered properly dressed.

Peng looked admiringly at Lansee's gleaming black hair wound in a large bun on top of her head. Her smooth skin shone like bright copper, and tiny earrings of soft gold sparkled in the sunlight when she tossed her head at him teasingly. Although she was friendly with everyone, she managed to stay near him.

He brought her some rice and pork on a banana leaf and she ate delicately. Then they joined their friends around a large jar of rice wine, taking turns drinking from one of the many bamboo straws protruding from the jar. Throbbing music from drums, cymbals and reed flutes filled the air.

Several hours later, Peng and Lansee were sitting under a tree, laughing and joking. Peng had drunk much rice wine, and everything appeared hazy to him except her smiling face as he heard himself telling her things he had never shared with anyone else.

Suddenly she looked up, and froze. The smile slipped from her face. Someone in the darkness grabbed her hand and pulled her to her feet, shouting angrily. Peng struggled to focus his eyes and tried to stand, but she had disappeared into the night before he could recognize who was dragging her away.

Later he could only vaguely remember stumbling through the village to get home. His sleep was restless and troubled, and when he awoke the next morning he still burned with anger and humiliation.

He returned to the feast that afternoon determined to find Lansee and ask who had taken her from him. But she never appeared.

While the boisterous merrymaking continued, Samat and another village priest went into the forest to make a second offering to the spirits. Carefully choosing an area where a certain spirit was known to reside, they placed on the ground a bamboo fetish representing a water buffalo, and blessed it with magic incantations. They hoped to deceive the spirits into believing a live animal was being sacrificed, for water buffaloes were valuable animals needed to plow the fields before each rice planting. If all the people now ill with fever recovered, then a real buffalo would not have to be killed. Everyone hoped the blood from the pig sacrificed yesterday would be enough to satisfy the spirits and bring an end to the sickness.

Peng sat for hours at the edge of the noisy crowd, eating little and struggling with his disappointment. Anger and bitterness flared up within him as he saw the other young men enjoying themselves and taking little notice of him, except for Heng who glanced at him several times with a knowing smirk. Peng finally stood up and started toward him, determined to challenge Heng and discover whether he knew what had happened to Lansee.

"Sit down!" a voice said gruffly. Peng blinked and saw Khap standing in front of him.

"Don't make a fool of yourself," his brother said. "Leave Heng and the others alone. They are all drunk. You'll only start a big fight if you ask them about Lansee."

Angrily, Peng pushed his brother away. "Leave me alone! I've got to talk to Heng." He turned toward the crowd of young men. But Khap grabbed his arm and pulled him back, throwing him to the ground.

"What's wrong with you?" Khap knelt at his side, whispering angrily and shaking him. "You know you'll be in serious trouble if you start a fight during the feast. Get that wild gleam out of your eyes. You must learn to control your temper, Peng."

"But Lansee . . ." Peng spluttered, unable to put his fears into words.

"Everyone knows Lansee has been kept home from the feast today. Somehow she has displeased her parents. Maybe they don't want you to be their son-in-law."

Peng stared at his brother in the fading light. Everyone knew he had been rejected? How could he bear the shame? If only he could go to Lansee's house and talk to her! If he had offended her parents, he would apologize. Surely they would listen to him.

A Taway girl was usually allowed to select her own mate even though her parents disapproved of her choice. Had Lansee given in to pressure from her family? Or did she want someone else after all?

Peng sat on the ground, his head in his hands. He would not give in so easily. Although it was contrary to their tribal customs, he would approach her parents tomorrow. Lansee was special, and he knew he would never want any other girl.

"Let's go home," he groaned unhappily. Khap walked back to the house with him, trying to cheer him up, but Peng said very little. No one must know of his plans, or they might interfere. He pretended to be resigned to his fate.

"Go on back to the feast, Khap. I'll be all right now," he said as he began to climb the ladder to the empty house. Khap hesitated, then disappeared into the darkness.

Dejected but determined to regain Lansee's favor, Peng sat for several hours on the verandah, planning what he would say to her parents. The only sound was that of the wind ruffling the leaves of the tall palm trees above him and the shrill song of the cicadas.

Suddenly a rock struck him on the shoulder, two others bouncing off the wall of the house. He heard scuffling footsteps below him. "Who's there?" he cried.

"Leave Lansee alone," a voice called out of the night. "Otherwise you will be killed."

Peng leaned over the edge of the verandah. Was that Heng's voice? He was not sure. He could see no one below in the inky darkness, but he thought he heard someone running away. He shivered in spite of the warm night, knowing this was no idle warning. Perhaps someone had already put a curse on him. Such threats were common among the Taway people, and mysterious deaths often followed. Although he thought Lansee loved him, evidently someone else was determined to be her husband.

He went inside the dark house and groped his way to the mat in the corner where he usually slept. Sitting with his chin resting on his bent knees, he thought about the warning. He hadn't been able to recognize the voice. He frowned, trying to remember who else had visited Lansee's grass hut during the courting time. Each harvest season the teenage girls slept in small makeshift huts in the cleared fields. Nearly every evening Lansee's hut had been surrounded by eager young men singing and playing music to attract her attention. Several others had won her favor before she had noticed him and invited him into her hut. He had slept in several girls' huts in the past, but now he could think only of Lansee.

Loneliness pressed on his heart like an icy stone. He loved children and longed to have a family of his own. "Will I ever find a wife?" he wondered. Some of his younger friends were already married. He was now 23 years old, but thus far no one had chosen him, perhaps because he was often shy one minute and hot-tempered the next. Or was it because he was expected to become a spirit priest like his father? Lansee's friendliness had seemed to fill a void in his heart. Usually he couldn't think of much to say to girls, but he had felt relaxed with her.

Peng stared into the darkness, wondering if his enemy would really try to kill him if he ignored the death threat. Being the son of a spirit priest was of some value, of course. Everyone knew his father could divine the cause of illnesses, ward off curses and appease the spirits with the proper offerings. But people did not fear Samat, for they knew he was unlikely to cause death or sickness in revenge. Samat was not power-hungry like some of the other village priests. He truly loved the Taway people and in return was highly regarded.

Peng had always been proud of his father's occupation and had even looked forward to following in his footsteps. But now he wondered what advantage there would be in becoming a *shaman*. It meant surrendering himself completely to the demons, obeying their directions in every tiny detail. He would appear to have power, but actually he would be in bondage to the world of invisible spirits. People would respect him outwardly but deep down in their hearts they might fear him. Was this the kind of a life he wanted?

Peng finally lay down on his mat, but he could not close his eyes. He thought about what Khap had said. Could it be possible that sickness and trouble did not come from the evil spirits? If that were true he did not need to become a priest and serve the spirits. He could live a normal life. Perhaps then Lansee would have the courage to declare her love for him in spite of her family's wishes. Or was she just a fickle flirt like so many of the other girls? Waves of bitterness swelled up inside him, almost drowning his grief and anger.

It was a long time before he dozed off. His sleep was restless, broken by dreams of fierce faces and the sensation of being pursued by an evil power. He awoke in a sweat, his heart thudding.

His father was bending over him. "What is it, son? You were shouting something." Peng sat up in the darkness and shook his head, trying to clear his mind. He trembled when he recalled that something evil had been chasing him.

"I just had a bad dream," he said, determined not to tell his father about the death threat. He would handle his problems by himself.

Sensing something deeper, Samat finally persuaded him to describe the dream. "It felt as if the spirit of death was chasing me," Peng concluded. "Does that mean I am going to die soon? What happens to us after we die? Do we join the evil spirits that torment the living?"

His father nodded. "The spirits of the dead have great power over us. That's why we must be careful to appease them."

Peng's heart chilled with fear. There was no comfort in such beliefs.

3

Escape From Death

LATE THE NEXT morning Peng and Khap went down to the fields to thresh the remainder of the rice. For several hours they stomped about on the threshing area in the hot sun, separating the rice grains from the stalks with their feet. Peng was glad he didn't have to do the job barefooted as his grandparents had. Samat sometimes wore leather foot coverings made especially for threshing time, but his sons preferred the canvas shoes they bought in the nearby town.

Khap joked and tried to cheer up his brother, but Peng would not respond. His thoughts revolved in a bitter circle, tormenting over and over, "You've lost Lansee. You'll never find a good wife. You've lost Lansee. You'll never find a good wife." He realized that probably everyone knew Lansee had rejected him. Juicy news like this would spread quickly through the village.

There was no enjoyment in working together that day, so the brothers quit early. Peng went home and lay listlessly on his mat in a dark corner of the house, more exhausted by the endless circle of his dismal thoughts than by his physical labors. He decided to wait until after supper to visit Lansee and her parents.

His mother and sister came in and began to prepare the evening meal. Talking cheerfully, they tried to rouse him, but he rolled over on his side, rudely turning his back to them. Women don't understand how they can hurt a man, he thought grimly. They lead a man on and then drop him. Bitterness flooded his heart. Would he ever trust a woman again? He tried to work out a way to confront Heng privately, but his thoughts seemed jumbled and confused. He knew he could not act until Khap left, anyway, lest he try to interfere.

That evening everyone ate in gloomy silence, weighed down by Peng's obvious unhappiness. Then Khap dropped his bombshell.

"Pa, I'm going back to the city and stay awhile," he said.

Samat reached for a handful of rice, trying to stay calm. He looked sternly at Khap, his thick eyebrows and unruly thatch of black hair appearing to bristle with anger.

"How long will you be gone? Do you have to go now when we need you here?" Samat fought to keep his gruff voice from quavering. He sensed he was losing his youngest son but he didn't understand why.

"I'll be away several months, I guess." Khap tried to speak nonchalantly. "The threshing is nearly finished now, anyway."

Samat's gaze traveled to Peng's bowed head and back to Khap's determined face, asking a silent question.

"Oh, Peng will recover," Khap shrugged. "There are other girls in the village. He wouldn't laugh at my jokes today, and I can't make him smile if he wants to be miserable. I've got to get away from this wretched village where everyone is either sick, sad, or scared to death of the demons. I can become somebody in the city, but here I'll never amount to anything."

Without waiting for his father's answer Khap got up and left the room. The next morning he slipped away before sunrise, unwilling to face his parents' arguments or their tearful farewells.

Peng didn't go to Lansee's house after all. Fear that a curse would be put upon him had sapped his resolve. Despair overwhelmed him and convinced him that he had no hope of marrying Lansee.

During the following week Suk noticed that Peng ate very little, although he was working hard. After a few mouthfuls at mealtime he would turn away to sit alone on the porch, unwilling to speak to anyone. His mother was very concerned, for he usually had a hearty appetite.

No one else died of fever that week; it seemed the spirits were satisfied. The nights turned cooler as the dry season progressed, and Suk got out the rest of their blankets. They had more than most families, but still the cold nights were uncomfortable. Many of the village children had coughs and runny noses. Peng developed a sore throat, and sores broke out on his legs and feet.

He managed to keep Lansee out of his thoughts most of the time, but now his mind was filled with a thirst for revenge. He heard that Heng was seeing her regularly, and this increased his anger. Finally he had a plan worked out. He would go to Heng's house in the evening and fight him if necessary; that would show he wasn't afraid of his threats.

But that afternoon Peng came home from the fields with a high fever and lay down immediately, unable to eat. During the night he became violently ill. Samat chanted over him until dawn and offered a chicken to the spirits the next morning. But Peng became worse and was delirious all day, tossing wildly in his sleep, groaning and shouting.

Samat sacrificed his biggest pig that evening and renewed his vows to serve the spirits more faithfully if only they would spare his son. He didn't know what else to do. Through the long night he sat anxiously beside Peng, chanting constantly as Suk hovered nearby. They had lost several children during infancy, and now had only four left. Their older daughter Noy was already married. But now Khap had left home, and Samat's heart constricted with fear as he watched his firstborn fighting the fever.

At dawn Peng lay very still, barely breathing. Then he opened his eyes slowly, sighed, and asked for a drink of water. Soon he was asleep again, breathing naturally.

When he awoke in the afternoon he was hungry, and eagerly devoured the delicious *keng* his mother offered him. Although he felt weak for several days, gradually his strength returned. However, often he would awaken in the night with a feeling of fear and depression. If only he could become a better person! He was ashamed of his temper and his habit of sulking when he was angry. No wonder girls didn't like him. He knew he deserved to die and be punished by the evil spirits.

One morning soon after Peng's recovery, Samat went into the forest and chopped down a piece of large bamboo which he cut in half, making two hollowed-out tubes. He carried these home and put them beneath the house. "We must collect your soul spirits so you will be completely well again," he told Peng. Like the Lao, the Taway people believed each person had 32 spirits, one for each part of his body. When someone fell asleep it was because some of his spirits had wandered away, and if they did not all return he would become ill and die.

When the sun was high above the village Peng took a handful of uncooked rice from a basket in the house and followed his father down the ladder outside. Samat had woven some small pieces of split bamboo into special magic patterns. He spread the bamboo designs on the ground and then Peng sprinkled the rice on them. The food should encourage the hungry spirits to return. Calling his spirits by the names his father had taught him, Peng picked up the bamboo tubes and waved them slowly from side to side, then quickly corked the ends with plugs of straw to trap his soul spirits inside.

Afterwards they carried the tubes and woven patterns into the house, where Samat began to chant and call on the spirits to stay with his son. Carefully he uncorked each bamboo tube, holding it close to Peng so all his soul spirits would return to his body.

That evening Peng's friends came to wish him good health. They sat in a circle around him, as a pile of freshly chopped pine chips burned slowly on a large flat stone set at one end of the clay firebed, where supper had been cooked an hour before. The dim light flickered on their faces as one by one the young men came forward and tied short cotton strings about Peng's wrists.

"May you be as strong as the antlers of a stag, the jaws of a wild bear, or the tusks of an elephant!" Bek smiled at his cousin as he chanted, tying a string carefully on each of Peng's wrists.

"May everything yield before you and may you be free from want!" another friend said.

Samat came forward and tied two long strings around his son's chest. "In our language your name means long life. May you live a thousand years, and may you have abundant riches of every kind," he chanted. "May you always have strength to stand for what is right."

Soon both Peng's wrists were covered with thick bracelets of cotton strings, but his friends continued to come forward with their blessings.

"Should you suffer with fever again, may it disappear quickly."

"May you have long life, health, happiness and strength."

Suk and Ying came forward with their good wishes and then passed around a plate of bananas for the guests. They lit several fresh pine chips, and the light flared out into the dark corners of the sooty rafters, illuminating each smiling face as Peng's family and friends celebrated the safe return of all his soul spirits. The fragrant aroma of pine smoke mingled with the musty odors of the simple tribal home.

Death seemed far away from the room filled with laughter and good will. Peng's heart rejoiced as he looked around at his friends and felt new health and strength coursing through his body. It was good to be alive! He decided it was better to be content with his recovery than to risk losing his life by trying to regain Lansee's love. Her beautiful face and the events of the feast had already become dim in his memory, but he knew the curse was real. It might not be overcome so easily next time.

Late the next afternoon Peng was resting on the verandah, watching his father skillfully weave a new fish net from the strong cotton thread his mother had made that winter. The tightly woven mesh grew steadily under the quick movements of Samat's fingers. Peng stirred restlessly. The air was heavy and humid with no hint of a breeze. It seemed unusually warm for the dry season.

At last the blazing sun dropped out of sight, leaving streaks of red and gold across the sky. Samat put his weaving aside as dusk crept across the village and a light breeze began to ruffle the fronds of the papaya trees and tall coconut palms overhead.

"It's good to be well again," Peng said, looking at his father gratefully. "I'm glad I have a father who knows how to bring healing."

Samat recalled how inadequate his chants and offerings had seemed when Peng was on the edge of death. "There are many illnesses I don't understand," he admitted. "Sometimes it's difficult to know which spirit has sent the sickness. But I do what I can to help my people."

He looked at Peng and sighed. "It's not easy serving the spirits. They require complete obedience in every detail. I'm always afraid I'll forget some taboo and anger them."

Peng nodded as he recalled the foods his father wasn't allowed to eat, the special places he couldn't go in the forest, the particular ways he was required to behave in his own house.

"Fear is all about us," Samat said. "The evil ones have supreme power."

Peng looked up at the star-filled sky. "Do the evil ones also control the stars, the moon and the sun?"

Samat shrugged his shoulders. "I don't know. Those things never change in their patterns. The stars and the moon follow their usual courses month after month. The sun rises each morning whether we have trouble or prosperity. Sometimes a refreshing rain comes even when the spirits are punishing us with sickness."

Peng had been wrestling with many questions since his illness. He knew he had almost died and had miraculously escaped the power of the evil ones, but someday he would face death again. Was there no escape from the spirits? Then he remembered an ancient legend passed on by the old men of the village.

"Tell me the story of the rock flowers again," he asked. The lichen which grew on the boulders in their fields and villages was called rock flowers by the Taway.

"Many years ago the Great Spirit was drawn into a battle with the seven bad spirits who chased Him away. Our ancestors then turned their attention to appeasing the evil spirits, and they forgot who the Great Spirit was and even lost His name. But one day the Great One will return, and as a sign of His coming the rock flowers will begin to enlarge and become brighter and more obvious. Until then we must continue to serve the bad spirits and not speak evil of them, lest they destroy us."

Peng considered his father's words. If only the Great Spirit would return soon! Perhaps He was the one who had made the earth and the beautiful things in it. Surely He would deliver him from the terrible fear that gripped his heart.

A few weeks later Peng heard that Lansee was expecting a child. He waited anxiously to see whom she would name as the father, although he had no hope he would be chosen. She avoided him in the village, and he had not spoken to her since the night of the feast.

When he learned that Lansee had chosen Heng, he finally understood why Heng hated him. He had wanted Lansee for his wife. Peng's heart swelled with bitterness against his former friend. He couldn't forgive him for taking Lansee. Heng must have been the one who sent the warning the night of the feast. Who else could it have been? Lansee's father? He would never know, but it was too late to matter now.

About that time a young mother died in childbirth. In accordance with tribal custom, her healthy baby was buried with her. The father had no one to help him raise the child, and the *shaman* he consulted recommended that he appease the angry spirits by giving up the baby to them. This angered Peng. He knew he would have been terribly grieved if Lansee and his own child had been the ones to die. Why were the spirits so cruel to demand the life of a living baby? Wasn't it enough that they took the mother?

Surely there was a better way than this, Peng thought. Slowly a resolve formed in his heart to search for deliverance for his people.

4

The Search

THE MARKETPLACE IN town was still crowded when Peng arrived, for he had left his village before dawn. Because of his recent illness, he felt more tired than usual from the three-hour walk. But his hearty appetite had returned, and his stomach growled with hunger. He decided to find something to eat before trading the bananas, tobacco, and chili peppers he had brought with him.

Coughing frequently and feeling chilled in spite of his long walk, Peng strolled across the open square where food was arranged on the ground in neat rows. Farmers from the country-side had brought in baskets of rice, peppers, bananas, papayas, bamboo shoots, and other items. Live chickens squawked inside loosely woven reed cages as women bargained for them in shrill voices. Peng didn't have a permit to sell in the marketplace, but he knew a shopkeeper who would probably buy from him.

Recognizing a friend from a neighboring village, he stopped to admire the pile of frogs and small fish he had for sale. Fresh fish were not often sold in the market, because everyone in Laos enjoyed fishing and caught their own, making *padek*[1] when they had an overabundance, to carry them through the periods when fish was scarce.

"Has fishing been good in the rivers and ponds, uncle?" Peng asked respectfully as he squatted down beside the elderly man. Shaking his gray head sadly, the man described how difficult it was to catch anything but frogs because of the long drought. When the monsoon rains began in April the fishing would improve, but that was two months away.

After discussing the poor harvest and other news with his friend, Peng excused himself and wandered to the other side of the marketplace where a Vietnamese man was cooking noodle soup over a small charcoal fire. This was very different from the food he ate at home, but he had developed a liking for it during the years he had been coming to town. Often there was no other cooked food available at the market, and after the long walk from his village he craved something more than a mango or coconut.

A bowl of noodles cost five *kip*[2] but the man agreed to accept several bananas as payment. Peng then squatted down and took the bowl of steaming soup and the chopsticks that were handed to him. He didn't really know how to eat with chopsticks, but he copied the other customers

---

[1] Fish preserved whole in salt along with ricebran.
[2] A *kip* is the smallest unit of Laotian money; 100 *kip* equaled about US$1 at that time.

who were noisily eating their soup nearby. He held the bowl up to his lips and shoveled the noodles into his mouth bit by bit with the chopsticks, occasionally taking a sip of the savory broth. It made his sore throat feel much better.

He noticed a Huay tribesman eating nearby, and this reminded him of a strange experience he had had several months ago. A Huay man who had squatted down to eat beside him at the market one day had first bowed his head and begun to talk with his eyes closed. His language was similar to Taway and Peng caught the meaning of a few words expressing thanks.

"Who are you talking to?" he had finally asked. The man had replied simply, "God made the earth and everything in it; therefore we should thank Him before we eat."

Peng had puzzled over this many times. He knew that some spirits were not unkind to men, but they never claimed to have created the world! They were aloof, uninterested in humans, although generous animal sacrifices could persuade them to keep the evil spirits in check. According to some traditions men had lived inside the earth until they found a hole and climbed out onto the surface. No one knew where the earth had come from. Perhaps the Great Spirit of the rock flowers had created all things. But who was He, and how could a person find him?

Peng wished he had been in Khang village the time when some Huay men who lived on the mountain had challenged the Taway to follow the "true God." Each tribe had its own spirits to worship; why did those men feel their God was the only true one?

After he finished eating Peng went to one of the many small shops that bordered the market square. He had traded at this one frequently, and the shopkeeper knew him by name.

"Peng! *Sambai baw!*[3] Are you well?" The owner came forward with a smile, carrying his small daughter on his hip. Peng could hear a baby crying in a room at the back where the family lived.

"*Sambai dee!*"[4] he answered. "I've been very sick but am better now. Is your family well?"

"Yes, we are fine," the shopkeeper nodded. "Our children were sick, but the foreigners at the clinic gave them medicine and they have recovered. You have a bad cough," he observed.

"Oh, nearly everyone in my village has a cold. Several people have died," Peng reported. "Our spirit medicine didn't work for them."

"The Filipino doctor here in town has powerful medicine, and it's not expensive. He is friendly and kind; don't be afraid to go to him. He has helped many people since the clinic opened last month."

To be polite, Peng asked, "Where does he live?" He paid little attention to the answer, for he was sure he wouldn't try any foreign ways.

---

[3] The traditional Laotian greeting, literally "Are you well?"
[4] The customary response, literally "I am very well."

He put a large bundle of tobacco on the wooden counter beside his basket of bananas and chili peppers. He had grown the red and green peppers in his garden and carefully dried them in the sun.

"I want a kilo of salt and one of those blankets," he stated, pointing to a thick brown blanket on a high shelf.

"That's worth three hundred *kip*," the shop-keeper protested.

"But I have two kilos of tobacco here. You know our Taway tobacco is the best," Peng insisted. "And these peppers and bananas are worth a hundred *kip*."

After a few minutes of good-natured bargaining they agreed on a price, and Peng left with the blanket, a small bundle of salt, and also ten *kip* cash.

He strolled along the street feeling pleasantly satisfied with his purchases. His people could provide nearly everything they needed for themselves from their gardens, the rice fields, and foraging in the jungle, but it was often difficult to find salt in the woods, and their looms were too narrow to weave blankets. Peng didn't like to be dependent on those outside his tribe, but he had learned to enjoy bargaining for things in town.

It was still early in the day and he was feeling tired, so he decided to go down by the riverside to rest in the shade before returning home. Walking along an unfamiliar street, he paused a few minutes later beside a fence which had a sign on it in large round Laotian letters. He stared at the words but couldn't decipher the meaning. Having attended school for only a few weeks many years ago, he had never learned to read very well.

Coughing again, he had turned and started to walk on, when suddenly a woman came out through the open gate and called to him. "Don't be afraid!" she said. She spoke in Lao but something seemed different about her speech. Looking back at her Peng noticed that although she had brown skin and black hair like a Laotian, her hair was not twisted into a bun on top of her head but was short and wavy.

"I heard you coughing. Would you like to see the doctor?" she asked. "He could give you some medicine. Come, I'll show you the way."

Peng didn't know what to say, but he couldn't rudely walk away. So after a moment's hesitation he followed her through the courtyard and into a small building, still coughing. His throat did feel much worse. This must be the Filipino clinic, he thought. Perhaps it would be all right to try the foreign medicine.

He stood in the doorway, looking about him, and noticed there were several tables and chairs in the room. These people must be wealthy, he decided. Only government officials or the very rich had such things in their houses.

A dark-skinned young man in white clothing came toward him. "Come sit here and let me look at your throat," he said kindly.

Peng laid his bundles down and sat awkwardly in the chair. He would have been more comfortable sitting on the floor. The man put a thin piece of wood on his tongue and peered into his mouth, asking him to repeat a grunting noise. Then with an odd-shaped instrument in his ears, the doctor placed the other end of a long rubber tube on his chest, frowning as he moved it about. Peng wondered what he was doing. Could he tell if all his soul spirits had come back into his body?

The doctor spoke to the woman who was watching, and she brought him a small envelope. He opened it and showed Peng the little pills inside.

"Swallow one of these every morning and evening for ten days," he said. "Then if you are still coughing, come back and I'll give you more."

Peng held out his ten *kip*. "This is all the money I have," he said.

"Six *kip* is enough," the doctor answered, giving him four crumpled bills in change. "Even if you don't have money, come back if you need more medicine. It may help the sores on your legs as well as your cough."

Peng left the clinic with many questions tumbling in his mind. Was it right for him, the son of a spirit priest, to eat the foreigner's medicine? Although the Filipino doctor looked like a Laotian, Peng suspected that his country was far away. His customs and religion must be quite different, so how could his medicine help people in Laos? Laotian ways were not good for the Taway people, so how could the foreigner's ways be good for him?

More than the healing of his cough and the sores on his legs, Peng longed for deliverance from his fear of death. His heart felt troubled and heavy whenever he thought of the future. Was there no way to find happiness in this life or after death?

He suddenly recalled what he had heard long ago from his friend Wen, a Lao boy who lived in a village near the motor road. Wen had once spent three months in the Buddhist temple earning merit for his family. When Peng had asked what he should do to enter the place of eternal bliss, Wen had told him to *het boun*[5] by lighting candles in the temple, bringing flowers and food and other gifts to the monks. A person could make extra merit by studying in the temple for several months or years and by fasting and denying himself and observing the Eight Precepts of Buddha. If he earned enough merit, he might be born as a rich or wise person in his next life and after many re-incarnations attain the cessation of desire and personality and thus reach Nirvana.

Peng was thinking hard as he stopped to rest in the shade of a large mango tree near the edge of town. The Buddhist teachings made salvation seem very difficult and uncertain. However, maybe he had misunderstood Wen. Perhaps a monk at the temple could explain things better.

---

[5]Literally, make merit. Most Lao boys spend several months in the Buddhist temple at some point in their lives, often just before marriage.

Surely there was a way to find relief from the misery in his heart? He hesitated, then turned around and followed the street which led to the temple.

Inside the courtyard he found a young monk meditating under a flame tree, surrounded by bright red blossoms which had fallen to the ground. Peng bowed respectfully to the monk in his saffron-colored robe.

"Sir, please tell me, can I earn salvation by following the teachings of Buddha? I feel very burdened by my sins."

The monk explained what was required to enter the place of heavenly bliss. "Anyone can earn some merit by self-denial and good deeds. But you must study and pray for a long time to earn enough to outweigh the volume of all your sins. If you became a monk for a few years, perhaps you might be born into a Lao family in your next life," he told Peng. "But it takes many lifetimes of meditation and good works even for a Laotian to earn enough merit to enter Nirvana."

Peng finally turned away in sorrow. Apparently even the Lao had no certainty of salvation. As he walked home reflecting on the monk's words, anger began to boil up within him. He was proud to be a Taway and didn't want to become a Laotian. They despised the tribal people who felt that blood sacrifice was necessary to appease the spirits of the forest. Laotians thought they were better than the tribes because they didn't shed blood! But they would buy meat in the market from others who had killed the animals. They acted very self-righteous, but Peng suspected they were sinners just like tribal people. He wondered if anyone knew how to find peace of heart.

At last he turned from the hot dusty motor road onto the path which led through the jungle to his village. When he came to a large flat rock he sat down to rest. It was pleasant sitting under the trees, shaded from the hot sun. He had known this trail since he was a child, and the dense forest stirred no fears within him.

Suddenly he saw a strange figure on the path before him! He was horrified to realize that its face resembled his own, but it had a body like a pig. Revolted, he sat motionless and terrified as the creature slowly approached. Then it mysteriously disappeared, leaving him trembling with fear, his skin clammy with sweat. He jumped up and ran down the path, not stopping until he had left the jungle and was crossing the sun-scorched paddy fields outside his village.

★   ★   ★   ★

The next day Peng took the new blanket and some salt to his uncle Vahn who lived alone in an old granary near the river. Vahn faithfully tended the family garden there during the rainy season, but now the ground was barren and dry. Vahn was crippled and had never married. His feet were twisted backwards so he had to walk on his knees, wearing pads he had made from old truck tires. Although he was busy making a knife for a villager with his blacksmith tools, he stopped when Peng arrived.

"Let's eat," he said, setting out a *keng* he had made that morning with some snake meat. Flavored with banana blossoms, it was quite delicious.

"You're a good cook," Peng complimented him, taking a second helping on his rice.

After they finished eating they sat on the narrow porch to relax. "Were there many people at the market in town yesterday?" Vahn asked.

"Not as many as usual," Peng replied. He described his visit to the clinic and added, "My father said I could eat the medicine and see if it would do any good. He thought the spirits wouldn't be offended if I didn't take it into the main village. Anyway, the medicine doesn't seem to involve worshiping a foreign god."

"If I had eaten the foreigner's medicine when I was a young man, perhaps my legs wouldn't have been crippled," Vahn replied. "The trouble started with sores on my feet just like you have. I made many offerings to the spirits but they never helped me."

Peng was silent for a long time. Then he said, "I had a strange experience on the way home yesterday." He described the frightening creature that had appeared to him on the forest path. "What do you think it means?"

"Oh," Vahn replied knowingly, "that is a sign the demons are ready for you to become a *shaman* like your father. As the eldest son you were sure to be chosen, but now they have given you a special mark of honor!"

Peng stared at his uncle in dismay. He wasn't at all pleased to hear this. Formerly he had been eager to become a spirit priest like his father, but since his illness he had been resisting the idea, because he saw that there was no freedom in serving the demons. His father's life was limited by many taboos. He couldn't eat the comb of a chicken nor the feet, which were a delicacy. Snake and monkey meat were also forbidden. More than that, Samat wasn't allowed to think or say anything contrary to what the spirits had taught the Taway for generations. Serving the spirits required complete submission.

The food taboos seemed a small sacrifice, but Peng wasn't willing to give up the right to think his own thoughts and search for the truth. Yet how could he find the truth? Was there any way to escape serving the evil spirits? Would he have to become a spirit priest like his father?

5

Discovery

O N THE WAY back to the village that afternoon Peng met his cousin Bek coming down the path.

"Peng, could you go to town with me tomorrow?" Bek asked. "Pak and Ling are going to carry some rice for me into Mong to sell, but I need your help, too."

"Of course I'll go with you, Bek!" Peng smiled at his cousin. Bek was a bit older than himself, but they had always enjoyed doing things together. "Maybe Lam will help, too, if I ask him," he suggested. Peng didn't really feel well enough to carry a heavy load of rice into town, but he wouldn't admit it. A Taway man never refused to help a friend or share with someone in need.

It was still dark the next morning when the five young men left the village, walking single file across the stubbled rice fields. By the time they had passed through the patch of forest and reached the motor road, the sky had brightened to a rosy pink. Like each of his friends, Peng carried a long pole balanced on one shoulder with heavy baskets of rice suspended from the ends. When the road turned east the fiery rays of the rising sun glared in his eyes and brought drops of sweat to his forehead.

Peng was still coughing frequently and feeling somewhat weak. The carrying pole with its heavy load cut into his shoulder, pressing him down. Powdery dust covered the motor road and billowed up around his feet as he trudged along in a slow jog behind his friends. Every year more dirt was pushed onto the road by the rains and winds of the monsoon season, covering the layer of gravel spread there long ago by the French. Occasionally a lumber truck passed them, grinding the earth into yet finer particles and leaving behind a suffocating cloud through which they plodded silently. Peng felt he was drowning in dust and he longed for the monsoon rains to arrive, although then the road would become a sea of mud.

When they finally reached town they sold their rice to one of the storekeepers for a good price and used some of the money to buy food. Peng bought a large piece of chicken that had been roasted on a bamboo stick. It had been brushed with a spicy sauce and had a delicious flavor.

Before returning home they strolled through Ban Tay, a small village on the edge of town near the river. Walking slowly along a shady path, they entertained themselves by peering into the shops, whose wide doors were unfolded to reveal a motley assortment of goods: woven baskets and bamboo mats, colorful enamel plates, salt, dried chili peppers, kerosene lamps, irregular cubes of yellow soap, metal buckets, and large tins of kerosene. A few shops also had blankets, skirts, and men's shorts for sale. The tribesmen were fascinated by the wares but they were reluctant to spend their money. Bek had given each one of them a few *kip* for helping him carry the rice to town.

Finally Pak stopped to buy a pair of shorts. As the others waited outside in the shade of a mango tree, they noticed a group of Lao soldiers eating at a small restaurant across the street. Seated at tables placed on the bare ground in front of the building, the soldiers were talking boisterously. Peng saw a young man eating alone in the dim interior of the cafe, and suddenly realized he was a Taway friend from a neighboring village.

"Is that you, Song?" he called out in surprise.

A grin of recognition spread over the young man's face. "Yes, it's me," he said, coming out into the sunlight. "What did you sell at the market today?" he asked, motioning toward their carrying poles and empty baskets.

"We sold ten baskets of rice," replied Bek. "The price is good this year. I'll be able to buy a young water buffalo now."

"The rest of us came to help carry Bek's rice," Lam explained. "I'm not going to sell much of my rice this year. I'd rather save it in case we have another drought."

"Bek doesn't have a family yet, but he'll have one soon," Peng commented with a laugh, poking his cousin in the ribs with his elbow. "He just got married and needs a water buffalo to plow with when planting time comes."

"Peng's father keeps him so busy he doesn't have time to start a family," Bek teased.

"Aw, he doesn't really want to get married, anyway. He scares all the girls away with his temper," jibed Pak, looking at Peng slyly, hoping to rile him.

Peng felt his face burn with embarrassment and anger. He clenched his fists and took a step toward Pak, ready to hit him. Bek put a hand on his shoulder and said quietly, "He's only teasing. Don't start a fight here, Peng."

An uneasy silence settled on the group. To change the subject Bek asked, "What are you doing here in town, Song?"

"I'm working for the white foreigner. Have you seen the tall fat man with the half-bald head?" The Taway men shook their heads and chuckled at Song's vivid description.

"I help with the marketing and cooking," Song explained. "The foreigner's wife is teaching me to cook so she can spend more time studying books and talking to visitors who come to their house. It's sometimes hard to follow her directions, because she doesn't cook like our Taway women do." He launched into a comical account of the foreigners' strange ways of doing things. The men seemed amused at this, so Song searched his memory for other details to entertain his audience.

"These people come from America," he said. "They teach a strange religion. The fat bald one says that if you believe in Jesus, their God, you'll never die but will live forever!"

Laughter rippled across the group as they acknowledged the foolishness of such an idea. The Lao soldiers eating nearby stared at the motley group of tribesmen chattering in their strange language. Some of the soldiers had only recently been transferred from towns in other provinces; they were unfamiliar with the tribes around Mong. They looked disdainfully at the uncouth tribesmen, then shrugged their shoulders and turned back to their food. They didn't have to be concerned about such riffraff as long as the men behaved and were loyal to the government.

Eventually Song ran out of humorous remarks. As Bek and his friends began to pick up their carrying pole and baskets, Peng asked Song, "Where do you live?"

"In a room behind the foreigners' house," Song answered. "It's right by the market, on the north side. Come visit me sometime."

On the way home Peng was quiet, puzzling over what he had heard. Why would Americans come to teach their religion in Laos? Didn't they know the Lao people had their own beliefs? A small group of American soldiers sometimes lived in Mong, but they didn't talk about religion; they were training the Laotians to fight against the communist rebels.

Peng decided the white man and his wife must be very brave to come into such a dangerous part of Laos. Although the town itself seemed safe, a battle could erupt at any time since there were enemy soldiers out in the forest everywhere.

Maybe the American thought he really would live forever! If so, he must have a strong God to protect him. Peng struggled in vain to remember the name of the foreigner's God. I'll visit Song again and learn more, he decided.

★   ★   ★   ★

Peng's cough was gone soon after he finished the medicine, but he still had sores on his legs and feet, and he ached all over, so he finally returned to the Filipino clinic in town for more medicine. This time the doctor gave him an injection, first explaining what he would do with the long needle. Peng gave his permission, but he was apprehensive as the doctor stuck the needle into his arm. However, it did not hurt much.

"You must return for several more injections," the doctor said. "Then the sores will disappear and you will be well again."

Afterward Peng went to the foreigners' house to talk to Song. Too timid to go up to the front door, he walked around to the backyard and found his friend behind the house roasting a fish over a small fire.

"Hello!" called Song in Taway when he noticed Peng standing at the gate. "Come in and eat with me."

Peng went into the yard and squatted down beside the fire. They talked quietly for a few minutes, then Song broke the fish in two and they ate it along with handfuls of cold rice from a woven basket.

Peng asked hesitantly, "Where is the American?"

"Oh, he and his wife follow the Lao custom of resting after their midday meal," Song explained. "They've been talking to visitors all morning, and they're tired."

"Tell me more about their God. What is His name?" Peng asked. "How do they worship Him?"

"His name is Jesus. They bow their heads and close their eyes when they talk to Him," Song said. "Sometimes they talk in their own language, but if I'm with them they talk in Lao. They say their God understands Taway, but they don't know how to speak our language yet. I'm teaching them some words."

"Do they offer chickens to their God?"

"No, they don't kill any animals for their religion, but *Than*[1] John told me he believes in blood sacrifice. He says God sent His Son Jesus to die in our place and that His blood paid for all our sins, so we don't need to offer chickens and pigs to Him."

"Have you talked to their God? What words do you say?" asked Peng eagerly.

Before his friend could answer, the back door opened and a large white man came around the corner of the house.

"Are you wasting time again, Song? Remember, I asked you to get some charcoal for us. If you wait any longer, they may run out like they did last

---

[1]Mr – a masculine title showing respect.

week." The American sounded cross but when he saw Peng he smiled and greeted him. "*Sambai baw*! Are you from Song's village?"

"No, I'm from Ban Dao," Peng replied, standing up. "I'd better go now." He hurried out of the gate and down the street before the American could reply.

The foreigner is very tall, Peng thought as he walked home. He's not really fat, just big and strong looking, and he has more hair than Song said. He wished he had not felt so timid before the white man; he should have stayed to learn more about the God named Jesus.

During the following week Peng turned over in his mind the things Song had told him. Could Jesus be the same God the Huay man in the market had been talking to before he ate his food? Could Jesus be the one who made the earth, sun and stars? I ought to thank Him for dying in my place, Peng told himself. But I don't know how to say the words or what I should do to follow His teachings. He decided he would go back sometime soon and learn more, although he felt nervous about approaching the big foreigner.

A few nights later Peng and several other young fellows were warming themselves around a fire near the center of the village, telling stories and jokes to entertain one another. Peng's uncle Loong and a friend joined them. Squatting down near the fire, they said they had visited the missionary's house that day.

"We heard him tell about Jesus at Ban Tee Village," said Loong, "and we wanted to learn more. He told us Jesus could set us free from the evil spirits!"

"Have you decided to follow this Jesus, then?" asked one of the young men.

"We were afraid," said Loong's friend. "Our wives aren't ready to believe. Will Jesus protect them? The missionary said we must not sacrifice to the spirits even to protect our wives and children. I don't want my family to suffer."

Peng listened intently but said nothing. Several in the group agreed it was too dangerous to forsake the spirits, even though the Jesus way sounded good.

But Loong said firmly, "When the missionary told us about Jesus, my heart felt he was saying the truth. How will we ever know for sure if no one is willing to try it? If I were a young single man free of responsibility, I would enter this religion. Aren't any of you young men brave enough to follow the Jesus way?"

The firelight flickered on their brown faces as the men looked at one another in silence. Several shifted themselves restlessly in their squatting position.

Peng thought in his heart, "I will follow the Jesus way." But he didn't have the courage to say it aloud.

6

Decision

PENG LEFT HIS village early the next morning as dawn streaked across the sky. The family was still asleep except for his mother, who was outside pounding the rice. He told her he was going into town to get another injection from the Filipino doctor, but didn't mention he also planned to visit the missionary. He was reluctant to discuss his errand with anyone because he knew what he had decided, and he didn't want anyone's advice. The early morning air was cool, so he wore the long dark trousers he had bought in town and a short sleeved shirt. Anyway, he wanted to look his best, for he felt this was a very important day in his life.

His feet were still sore, and he had to walk slower than usual, so the marketplace was nearly deserted when he arrived. The Vietnamese soupmaker had already left with his cart, and the few remaining people were hurriedly gathering their goods together, anxious to get out of the hot sun.

Peng was not interested in food today. He went to the clinic for his medicine and then headed straight for the missionary's house on the corner. Standing in the open doorway, he coughed softly to announce his arrival.

"*Sambai baw*!" a foreign lady came to the door and greeted him with a smile. "Come in," she invited. She was impressed by his neat appearance but couldn't decide what tribe he was from.

Peng stepped over the threshhold and looked around the large room. There were several chairs and a bench to his left. Colorful posters hung on the wall across the room.

"My husband isn't here right now," the woman said. "Do you want to hear about Jesus?"

He nodded and sat down in the chair, taking the piece of paper that she handed to him but not looking at it too closely. He felt very self-conscious talking to a foreign woman. If only the man would return soon! Women didn't know anything about religion.

"Look at the picture on the front," she was saying. "Oh!" she exclaimed, reaching out to turn the paper around. "Do you know how to read?"

Embarrassed, Peng shook his head. He had attended school only a few weeks in his early teens, and he was certainly not going to attempt to read in front of this foreigner! He looked at her doubtfully, wondering if she could read the Lao language.

"This picture shows the two ways men can go in this life," the woman explained, holding a booklet just like the one she had given him. "Most people follow this lower road of sin which leads to death and eternal punishment in hell," she said, pointing to the downward road which ended in flames of fire. She opened the booklet and began reading a description of man's rebellion against God.

Peng nodded as he listened. He didn't understand some of the Lao words, but he felt the tract was describing his own heart. He knew he was on the downward road. Fear and suffering were all the spirits had to offer. He stared at the small picture in his hands. There was another road going upwards, shining like bright sunlight. Was that the Jesus way?

"The upward path leads to heaven," she read. "God, who created all things, has made a way to come to Him. He sent His Son Jesus to show us the way . . ."

"Jesus! That's what I want," Peng interrupted.

The missionary looked up in surprise but then continued reading, "Jesus came down from heaven and lived in a human body so He could teach us about God. He taught that man is rebellious and deserving of death. Offering animal sacrifices cannot really take away sin. Jesus died in our place. He took our sins . . ."

"That's the name!" Peng turned to her with a bright smile. "Jesus," he repeated slowly. "I want to follow the Jesus way."

The woman was sure he didn't understand. He was probably just being polite and trying to please her. She gave him a puzzled look, and tried again to explain, "Jesus took our sins upon Himself, and became the perfect blood sacrifice, dying in our place. If you are willing to turn from your sins and trust Him, He will forgive you and give you eternal life."

"That's what I want," Peng declared eagerly.

She looked at him uncertainly, wondering if he could really have understood. She had never heard of anybody in Laos making such a quick decision to follow Jesus.

"Can you wait until *Than* John comes home?" she asked. "He can explain the Jesus way to you better than I can."

Peng nodded, so she brought out a small machine she said was a phonograph, and wound it up. It began to talk in Lao, and as he listened she sat quietly beside him.

At last the kitchen door swung open and they heard heavy steps. "I'll be back in a minute," the woman told him as she hurried out of the room. Soon the big foreigner came in and greeted Peng, pulled a chair over and sat down in front of him.

"My name is *Than* John. What's your name?"

"I'm Peng from Ban Dao, a Taway village at the foot of the mountains," Peng answered.

"I've never preached there," John said. "How did you hear about Jesus?"

"Song told me some things. Then my uncle and his friend heard you preach at Ban Tee recently. After they talked to you here yesterday they told me the Jesus way seemed good," Peng explained. "My uncle Loong would like to follow Jesus, but he's afraid the evil spirits might harm his wife and children. I don't have a family yet, and I want to enter your religion."

He looked at the white man anxiously. Did he understand?

"Do you know who created the world?" John asked.

"No," Peng answered. "I've heard there are good spirits, but we don't worship them. We don't really understand the spirit world, but our spirit priests tell us we must reverence the evil spirits so they won't harm us."

John said, "If you respect the evil spirits you will go to be with them after death. Do you want that?"

"No," Peng admitted. "They only want to torment us. I appease them only because that's what my parents taught me to do. If there's a better way I want to learn about it. I heard Jesus can help me."

"Who is Jesus?" John asked him.

"You yourself are Jesus," Peng said, feeling confused.

"No, I'm not Jesus," John said patiently. "Jesus is the true God, the creator of all things. He's in heaven, but His Spirit would come to be in you if you would believe in Him. Let me tell you about the one true God."

He explained that Jesus was the one who had created all things, and that He was a God of holiness and love. Peng struggled to follow the unfamiliar Lao words as the missionary explained how the first man had been tempted by the devil and had disobeyed God.

"That's how sin came into the world," John concluded. "Now everyone born into the world is a sinner. We have all chosen to go our own way, and none of us can do the things that please a holy God. I also am a sinner, but Jesus took my guilt on Himself and died in my place. He came back to life afterward and now gives me power to live a righteous life. He can do this for you too."

The missionary read from a thick book which he said was God's message translated into the Lao language. Peng listened carefully. If only the book spoke his own language!

Finally John asked, "Why do you want to follow Jesus?"

"Because His way is the right way," Peng answered quickly. "He created the world and He died for me. I know I am a sinner."

John looked at the young man's earnest face, then at the many strands of cotton strings around his wrists and the two strings tied around his chest. "Why do you wear those strings?" he asked, knowing they were related to pagan beliefs.

Peng explained, "After I was sick my friends put the strings on to wish me good health. They keep my soul spirits in my body."

"You must take the strings off if you truly want to follow the Jesus way," John said. "You can't serve Jesus if you are still obeying the evil spirits."

Peng hesitated. He suddenly felt afraid to make such a complete break with Taway tradition. He didn't want to get sick again. "I'll go home and get my belongings so I can live with you and study about Jesus," he said eagerly. "When I come back here I'll cut the strings off."

"You don't need to live here with us," John said kindly. "If you receive Jesus today you will be saved today. Remember the words we read in God's book? If you ask Jesus to forgive your sins and live inside you, He will be with you wherever you go. Jesus has greater power than the evil spirits, and He can protect you better than those strings can."

"Jesus will go with me to my village?" Peng was astonished. He looked down at the grimy strings tied about his wrists. "But what if something happens to me on the way home?" This foreign religion was very different.

"The spirits can't harm you if you are trusting in Jesus. But God won't be pleased if you keep on following the old ways. You must choose one way or the other." John took out his pocket-knife, opened it, and laid it on the chair next to Peng. "You must make your decision now. Maybe you won't have another chance."

Sweat broke out on Peng's forehead as he looked at the knife and hesitated. He began to tremble and feel very weak. For nearly ten minutes he sat in silence, counting the cost of breaking away from his old life. He did want to follow the true God. And since Jesus had created the world, surely He had greater power than the evil spirits.

"Will Jesus always be with me?" he asked.

"Will he help me whenever I ask Him?" The man nodded.

Peng's sweating stopped and he felt strength coming back into him. Slowly he picked up the knife and cut the strings, rolling them up in his hand.

Looking down at the crumpled strands he said, "Oh, Jesus, please help me. I want to be free from the evil spirits. You are greater than they are. Chase them out of my life! I'm trusting you to protect me from them and to forgive me for all my sins." With a great sense of relief he tossed the strings onto the floor behind him.

"I'll pray for you." When John bowed his head and began speaking to God as his heavenly Father, Peng's heart filled with wonder and joy. This God seemed so loving and under-standing! The foreigner talked as if Jesus were right in the room with them. As John prayed softly, Peng became confident that Jesus was really listening.

"Now thank God for saving you," John invited.

At first Peng hesitated, but then the words poured forth. "Oh God, you are the great one who created this world. Thank you for loving me. I know I'm a sinner. Thank you, Jesus, for dying in my place. Deliver me from the power of the spirits and help me to follow you always." He soon ran out of words but a feeling of peace and happiness swept over him. He looked up at the missionary, who smiled back at him.

"Now you're in God's family," John said.

"The path ahead won't be easy, but Jesus will always be with you. I want to visit your village sometime."

"I'd like that," Peng answered. "Ban Dao is really three villages – north, south and central Dao. I live in the northern part."

The woman, whose name he learned was Dorothy, brought a glass of water for each of them and sat down in a chair nearby. "*Kopjai*[1], Madam," Peng said gratefully before emptying his glass. It was near noontime now and the air was hot and still. He realized he was very hungry.

Suddenly the back door rattled as someone came inside. Peng looked up and saw his friend Song standing in the kitchen doorway holding a plucked chicken ready to cook. "Hello, Peng!" Song said in surprise. "Have you come to visit?"

"Yes," Peng answered. "I came to learn about the Jesus way, and I've decided to follow Him."

"Oh, I'm glad," Song said with a bright smile. "I've believed in Jesus, too, and now I won't be the only one from our tribe."

Dorothy stood up. "I must cook dinner now. We'd like you to stay and eat with us," she told Peng.

While she worked in the kitchen over the charcoal stove, John taught Peng some of the things he would need to remember in order to become a strong Christian. "The most important

---

[1] The Lao expression for "Thank you." Literally, "you grab my heart."

of all is to tell Jesus about anything that troubles you," he said. "Remember, He is all-powerful and can help you with any problems."

Peng was full of questions about leaving the old ways. He wondered what things he could eat and drink and what he should avoid.

John explained, "You can eat any foods you want, but rice wine is bad for your body. Be careful not to take part in any of the feasts that honor the evil spirits. Keep yourself pure for Jesus. Your people may be upset because you want to be different, but Jesus will help you to be brave and stand firm for Him. Tell them that Jesus loves each of them, too, and can deliver them from bondage to the spirits." John also gave him two small tracts. "Maybe someone can read them to you," he said.

The time went by quickly as John answered Peng's questions. When Dorothy called them to eat, they all sat down at the table. Peng, in a chair next to Song, bowed his head with the others when John thanked God for the food. Dorothy had prepared rice and a chicken *keng* which smelled good. She spooned some food onto each plate while Peng stared at the many unfamiliar objects on the table. Seeing John pick up a fork and begin to eat, he carefully followed his example. The food was delicious, and he soon began to relax and enjoy the meal. The foreigners were kind and hospitable, just like his own people, he decided.

"Come and see us often," they told him when

he finally left. His heart was filled with warm contentment as he set off down the road which led out of town. So many new ideas surged through his mind that he was hardly aware of the long walk home. He had many exciting things to tell his family and friends!

7

Declaration

As HE ENTERED his village late that afternoon
Peng heard a voice call, "Where have you
been today?" He looked up and saw his friend
Lam coming down the pole ladder from his house.

"I went to town to ask the American about
the true God," Peng answered. Stepping into
the shade under the house, he wiped the perspiration from his forehead with the back of
his forearm.

Lam joined him and asked, "Who is the true
God?"

"He's the one who created all things. His
name is Jesus, and I'm going to follow Him."

"You're going to follow the foreign God?"
Lam looked at him in astonishment. "The spirits
will be angry with you! You'll have sickness
and trouble."

"I've appeased the evil spirits all my life, but
still I've had much sickness. Jesus can protect
me. I've decided to follow His teachings, and
now I have peace in my heart instead of fear,"
Peng declared.

"How will you know the proper way to worship
Him? Are you going to live with the foreigners
and learn their language?"

"Jesus isn't just the God of the foreigners.

He loves all people everywhere," Peng replied. He tried to explain the wonderful things John had told him, but his friend only laughed.

"The foreigner's God isn't interested in us," Lam said. "You're foolish to leave the ways of our own people."

Peng's mother was cooking a chicken *keng* for supper when he got home. "Your father wants to talk to you. Why were you gone so long?" she asked crossly.

"I talked to foreign teachers in town about the true God," he answered as he sat down on a mat beside the fire. Suk looked at him sharply but said nothing. Peng watched her stir the *keng*. Orange hunks of pumpkin floated in the rich broth, making him feel hungry even though he had eaten with the missionaries only a few hours ago.

"Is the rice cooked yet?" he asked.

"Yes, go ahead and eat," she said, pleased that his appetite had returned. "Your father won't be home until late. He wanted you to go with him to south Ban Dao to see Pong. He's been very unhappy since his wife and baby died, and he was shouting and fighting with the villagers there today. He's asked your father to find out if someone put a curse on his wife to cause her death."

Peng's joy faded as he slowly ate his supper. He wanted to please his father, but he knew he couldn't participate in any more spirit ceremonies. He should not follow the old ways now that he had started on the Jesus path. He felt troubled, realizing that probably his father would be angry with him.

His little sister Ying came in and sat down on the floor beside him. Full of energy, she chattered happily about her day spent in the forest gathering nuts and bamboo shoots with her friends. Peng was fond of Ying but tonight he didn't pay much attention to her. He finished eating and went out on the verandah where he squatted down to wait for his father.

When Samat arrived the family gathered around him as he ate. "Pong is very upset," he told them. "He's threatened several people in the village. The ceremony I performed today didn't reveal who caused his wife to die, so I'll inquire of the spirits again tomorrow. I want Peng to go with me to help carry the magic stones."

"I can't carry the stones for you, father." Peng stared at the fading embers of the fire, his square jaw clenched with tension. His father waited in silence, and finally Peng looked up. "I've decided to follow the Jesus way, and I can no longer serve the evil spirits." He spoke quietly and respectfully, trying to control his natural tendency to argue and raise his voice.

"Who is Jesus? Can He protect you from the evil spirits?" Samat asked.

"Jesus is the creator of all things," Peng explained. "He is greater than the spirits, but He doesn't use His power to cause suffering and trouble. He loves everyone and wants to deliver us from bondage to the demons."

Samat looked at his son with a puzzled frown. "It would be good if that were so," he said finally, "but we know there's no escape from the demon spirits. Are you prepared to face their anger?"

Peng took a deep breath and looked at his father calmly. "I'm not afraid. Jesus is with me and will protect me."

Samat was speechless. Peng's temper often flared up easily, but he had never been obstinate. What had happened to make him so calm and determined to go his own way? Although Samat felt angry and disappointed that Peng had refused to help him, he struggled to keep a cool heart. He had found that the best way to control his sons was to keep them on a long leash and give them a fair amount of freedom.

"You don't need to come with me tomorrow," he said finally. "The spirits will listen to me better if you're not there thinking these new thoughts. However, you'll soon regret your foolishness. Our family may suffer much trouble because of your decision."

Samat's words haunted Peng that night. He was tired but couldn't sleep. He loved his parents and didn't want them to suffer.

"Oh, Jesus," he prayed, "protect my family from the anger of the demon spirits. Show them that you are all-powerful. Don't let the spirits punish them because I am following you. And please keep Pong from making trouble in the village."

He tried to recall some of the words from God's book. Jesus loves me, he remembered with a surge of joy. Repeating the beautiful name of Jesus to himself, he finally fell asleep.

When he awoke the next morning he sat up and thought, I didn't have any bad dreams last night. Surely Jesus is here with me!

He smiled at his mother who came in with the rice she had pounded. Quickly he piled dry twigs on the raised firebed in the center of the floor and blew on the hot ashes until bright flames shot up, licking at the half-burned logs left over from the night before. Suk hung the pot of rice on an iron hook above the fire and sat down in a corner to rest. Suddenly Peng realized she must be tired from rising so early to prepare the rice.

"You work hard, Ma," he said softly. "You're very good to us."

Suk smiled uncertainly at her son. Her family was fond of one another in the Taway manner but this was rarely put into words. Peng seemed different today.

The rice was ready to eat when Samat climbed the ladder and came in with Ying at his heels. "Pong came to see me early this morning," he said as Suk dished some rice onto his tin plate and set out several boiled chicken eggs and a saucer of hot peppers and salt. "He said it was fate that caused his wife to die, and he didn't want to accuse anyone. He seemed quite calm today." Samat glanced at Peng and saw he was smiling.

"Last night I asked Jesus to keep Pong from making trouble in the village, and already He has answered me!" Peng declared.

Samat frowned and began eating. Was it possible that this Jesus had accomplished what his charms could not do? He decided to watch his son and see if this new religion was as good as it seemed.

After breakfast Peng's young cousin Dee came by. "Lam says you have turned from the spirits to worship a new God. What will you do when they punish you with illness?" he asked.

"If I become ill, Jesus can make me well," Peng answered. "The missionary told me that sickness comes from something called 'germs', not from evil spirits. But even if the demons do attack me, I believe Jesus can deliver me from their power."

Uncle Loong was pleased when he heard that Peng had entered the Jesus religion. "I'll watch what happens to you, and maybe someday I'll follow Jesus, too," he said.

That afternoon Peng brought some bamboo from the forest to repair a weak place on the porch of the field hut. His friends Ling and Sahn came by as he was working.

"Is it true you have entered a foreign religion?" Ling asked. "Will you be coming to the feast at rice-planting time? We always have such fun together then!"

"No, I won't be coming to the feasts any more," Peng declared. "I'm following the Jesus way from now on, and I'm not going to appease the demons. They want to keep us in bondage and fear, but

Jesus is a God of love. He became the blood sacrifice for our sins so we could be delivered from the power of the spirits. Don't you want to be free, too?" He felt breathless after such a long speech, and his heart hammered with nervousness. Had he explained the Jesus way correctly?

"Of course, everyone wants to be free of the demons! But how can you be sure Jesus can overcome them?" Sahn looked at him doubtfully.

"I know it in my heart," answered Peng confidently. "I'm no longer afraid of the evil spirits. Jesus is the one who created the earth, the sun and stars, and all people. He sends the rain and makes the rice grow. We should worship Him, not the demons who hate us and always want to punish us."

He tried to persuade his friends to follow the Jesus way, but they shook their heads. "No, it's too dangerous to break away from the spirits, but we'll watch and see if Jesus protects you. We like to go to the feasts. You're going to be lonely if you don't come."

After his friends left Peng put his work aside and looked up at the sky. "Jesus, it's going to be hard to follow you. Please make me strong. Help me to show my people your way is the right way. Thank you, Jesus. I trust you and I know you're with me." Peace filled his heart as he prayed, and he felt much better. This is wonderful, he thought. Jesus really is here, and I'm not afraid.

When he returned home that evening he found the village filled with excitement and apprehension.

A large group of men were talking with his father outside the house. His cousin Bek was there and told him, "The governor has ordered ten of our men to meet at the edge of the south fields to-morrow morning. The rebel soldiers have attacked some villages north of Mong, and he wants us to cut some ironwood trees and build a bunker in his front yard."

"Why do we have to work for the governor?" a man complained loudly. "He's always asking us to do things for him. We pay our taxes. Last month we cut fence posts for him, and we have already sent five of our sons to join the Lao army!"

"That's right! We have our own work to do, and we are in danger, too," another man agreed.

An angry murmur rose from the crowd, but no one was willing to lead a revolt against the order. Finally the men agreed they would have to obey, and slowly the group dispersed.

The next morning Peng and Bek joined the group who were making their way to the woods beyond the south fields. Suddenly word began to go round that Peng had left the spirits. Tempers began to flare and he found himself at the center of an angry crowd. He saw that Heng had joined the men and was trying to stir up opposition to him.

"You can't forsake the spirits!" they shouted at him. "You'll bring their wrath down on our whole village."

"I've kept the way of the spirits all my life," replied Peng calmly. "I've eaten the flesh of sacrifice and drunk rice wine with you, but I've never been satisfied in my heart. I trusted in Jesus two days ago and now I'm already satisfied. You don't have to serve the evil spirits. Jesus can protect you from them."

"We don't want to leave the ways of our fore-fathers!" Heng cried. "We'll have only trouble if we follow the teachings of the foreigners."

"It'll be your fault if more sickness comes to our village," an elderly man warned him. "Don't you care about your own people?"

"I love my tribe," Peng answered. "Jesus loves all of you, too, and I'll ask Him to protect you from the power of the demon spirits. Someday you'll understand that the Jesus way is better."

With much grumbling and headshaking the other men finally scattered to hunt for ironwood in the forest, leaving Peng alone. At that moment *Than* John appeared from between the trees, wheeling his bicycle. "*Sambai baw*, Peng!" he called.

Peng's face lit up with a big smile as he saw his new friend. "Have you come to visit me already? I'm so glad to see you, *Than* John! Come with me into the forest. I have to cut ironwood trees for the governor today."

John followed him as he hunted for a suitable tree. Ironwood was very hard, quite difficult to penetrate with a small Taway ax, so Peng chose a fairly young tree. Even so as he hacked at it he made only slow progress, for he was still weak from his recent illness. He felt like swearing, but resisted the urge. When John insisted on taking a turn, he was glad to rest.

Finally Peng completed the undercut on one side. He leaned back on his ax handle, wiping the sweat from his face. Looking up at the sky he said simply, "Jesus, I don't know how to talk to you very well yet. But this is hard wood, and I'm not very strong. Please help me."

As they took turns chopping at the tree they talked about God's love and power. Peng thought *Than* John seemed worried about something.

Finally John said, "Peng, I came to tell you that we have to leave Mong on Saturday. We need to go back to America, because my wife Dorothy is not well. I'm sorry that we have to go right now, but she's been having chest pains for several weeks, and our mission doctor sent me a telegram yesterday saying that I should get her to a doctor quickly."

Peng was dismayed. "I'll be very lonely without you, *Than* John. I need someone to teach me more about God's way, because I don't understand it very well yet. But I'm sorry your wife is sick. It's right for you to go to America."

"We'll come back as soon as we can," John promised. "There's so much we want to teach you. God will make it possible for us to return, because I know He has called us to serve Him in Laos."

Peng asked what he meant by that, so John told him how he had promised to serve God if his mother was saved from a heart attack and how God had brought him and Dorothy together and called them to serve Him in a foreign land. "At first we didn't know where God would send us, but when we heard of the need among the tribes in Laos, we felt sure God wanted us to come here," John concluded.

"Weren't you afraid to go so far from your homeland to a country that is at war?" Peng couldn't understand why John would bring his wife to such a dangerous place.

"God has promised to be with us always, so we're not afraid. Jesus commanded His followers to take the good news of salvation into all the world, and He told us to come here," John explained.

"How did you learn to speak Laotian so well?" Peng asked. He was very curious about the foreigners.

"It didn't come easily," John laughed. "We've spent many hours studying the language with books and Lao friends to help us. Although Dorothy and I had already been engaged a long time, we postponed our wedding until after we had been in Laos two years, so we could concentrate on learning to speak Laotian. Also, I've been trekking back in the mountains near the South Vietnamese border where it wouldn't be safe for Dorothy to go, like among the Kasseng tribe."

"You've visited Kasseng villages?" Peng stared at John open-mouthed. "They used to *eat* people, and maybe they still do!"

"Yes, I know," John said, "but God kept me safe. No one there was willing to enter the Jesus way, but at least I was able to sow the seed of God's Word among several tribes. Now Dorothy is expecting our first child, and these chest pains might mean something is wrong with her heart, so I must take her to a doctor quickly. In a few months it would have been time for our furlough in America, anyway. But we will be praying for you while we are gone, Peng, and next year we will come back. Remember, you are not alone, because Jesus is with you."

8

Forgiven

APRIL WAS THE hottest month of the year. The ground felt scorched. Nothing could be done in the fields until the rains came to soften the earth, so Peng passed the long days relaxing in the shade. At least he felt good, for the sores on his legs had disappeared after several injections by the Filipino doctor. But he was bored with nothing to do, and most of his friends seemed to avoid him since his decision to follow Jesus. He wished the missionaries were still in town to teach him more about the true God. If only he had a copy of God's book and could read it for himself! He had tried to read the tracts John had given him, but he couldn't make much sense of them because of his lack of education.

Suddenly he had an idea. He sprang to his feet and hurried down the swaying pole ladder.

He found his friend Lam cutting strips of bamboo in the shade under his house, preparing to weave a new sleeping mat. Lam was actually a year younger than Peng but he seemed older, because he was already married and had one child.

"Would you teach me to read?" Peng asked him. "I'll help you plant your rice if you'll show me how to read Laotian."

Lam was surprised at this request, for the oldest son of a spirit priest was not encouraged to learn to read. His primary concern should be to preserve the traditions of the tribe. However, Peng was no longer interested in the spirit ceremonies, and he was old enough to make his own decisions.

"I can try to teach you what I remember," Lam answered hesitantly. "I have an old schoolbook we can use. When my father threw out my books years ago I hid one above the rafters in the thatch of our field house."

Together they walked down to the fields below the village, and Peng followed his friend into the bamboo hut. Lam went to a dark corner of the empty house and rummaged about in the dry thatch above the smoke-stained rafters. Finally he pulled out a small booklet, brushed off the dust, and handed it to Peng.

"Don't let anyone see it," he warned. "And don't tell anyone I'm helping you learn to read. You know how angry Kambit and the others would be."

Peng nodded in agreement. Kambit had led the spirit priests in convincing the people that bad luck would come to the tribe if their children learned the ways of the Laotians. Then the schoolhouse built for them by the government had mysteriously burned down.

"My brother taught me some words when he was going to school. I even sneaked over to the schoolhouse and sat in class for a few weeks before my father caught me," Peng said. "But I knew I was supposed to be in the forest guarding the water buffaloes. The teacher was always hitting my knuckles with a stick because I wouldn't pay attention, so I didn't like school."

The young men sat down near the door in a patch of sunlight and opened the book. "Does this say 'fish'?" Peng asked, pointing to a word on the first page under a picture of a fish.

"Yes." Lam turned the page and pointed to another sentence. "This says 'Father goes to the forest'. See, the words for 'fish' and 'forest' are almost the same. Just the tone is different."

Peng stared at the page and sighed. All the letters seemed alike unless one looked very closely. Laotian sounds weren't as beautiful as Taway words, but he was determined to learn to read and understand this language.

"Why do you want to read Laotian?" Lam asked.

"I want to study the book of Jesus' words that the missionary had in town," Peng explained. "When *Than* John read God's words to me my heart seemed to overflow with peace and joy. Someday I'll get a copy of God's book so we can read it together, but until then you could help me read the tracts *Than* John gave me."

Lam's eyes widened in apprehension. It might anger the spirits to show an interest in another religion. But when he saw the glow on Peng's face and his fearless determination, his heart softened. Glancing out of the doorway to be sure no one else was listening, he said, "I'd like to hear God's words. The way of the spirits is hard, and I don't have happiness in my heart. If you like, we can study together in your field house whenever we have some free time."

The weeks went by quickly after that. When Peng had a free hour he would go to the hut and study. Lam met him there often until Peng mastered the schoolbook and began learning to write.

At last the rains began to come more frequently. As each refreshing shower began, the children would run and splash in the puddles. Grown men stood carelessly in the rain to visit as they cooled off, and mothers took their little ones outside to bathe them.

It didn't take long to dry one's clothes, for the showers were short and the sun seemed hotter than ever afterwards. Steamy waves of heat rose from the wet ground. An hour later everyone's energy had evaporated in the high humidity and the paths through the village were nearly dry.

But there was little time to relax now. As the ground softened, much work had to be done in the fields to prepare them for planting. The Taway people grew their rice in paddy fields like the Laotians and had to have the dikes in good repair before the heavy monsoon rains began in earnest.

Most other tribes in Laos grew their rice on steep hillsides where the land could not be flooded. Between the eleventh and thirteenth centuries the tribes had been forced back into the mountains and hills along the eastern borders of the country when the Laotian race, originating somewhere near Tibet, had resumed its migrations and come down from Yunnan, China, to occupy the rich lowlands.

In their struggle for survival in the mountains many of the Mon-Khmer tribes had developed a slash and burn method of clearing a hillside for planting. First the large trees were taken to build houses and dugout canoes, and then the brush remaining on the hillside was burned. A grey haze hovered over the jungle for weeks during the burning time.

When rain had softened the earth, the rice was planted in holes dug with a sharp stick. The ashes left on the ground fertilized the crop as it grew. Sometimes this was a glutinous rice which the people cooked by steaming it in a bamboo container over boiling water.

Peng's tribe preferred ordinary rice boiled in a large pot. A proud people with a strong sense of independence, they had managed to retain their paddy fields in the lowlands even though in years past their ancestors had been forced to live on top of the mountain, nearly 4,000 feet above the plains, coming down only to plant and harvest their crops. Several generations ago they had returned to their villages near the foot of the mountain, but still they continued the practice of camping out in small huts in the fields during the planting and harvesting seasons. So each family had a small field house as well as a larger mountain home built among the boulders near the base of the mountain.

One night it rained hard for several hours, and the next morning at dawn Peng and his father walked out to the fields. They liked to work before eating their meal, while the air was still fairly cool. First they checked the dikes around each paddy and repaired the ones that were leaking. Several inches of water stood in the fields from the downpour in the night. When the ground was soft enough they would cultivate it with a wooden plow pulled by a water buffalo. Peng had heard that nowhere else in southern Laos were there such beautifully terraced fields. Terracing was not necessary on the plains where the Laotian grew their rice.

Using a hoe he had brought along, he dug up some weeds growing along the top of the dike. After clearing out several other patches of brush he stopped to rest. Looking around, he saw his father over near a fish-trap well chatting with their neighbors. In every direction stretched drab brown fields covered with muddy water. After the rice was planted and had begun to grow, the fields would become a brilliant green, and sparkle like a jade necklace lying along the base of the mountain. Those fields that contained fish holes would have a blue eye in the center where deep water sheltered the growing fish. Later at harvest time the rice would shimmer like gold in the sunlight; truly it was as precious as gold, Peng thought. Rice was not only the basic food of his tribe but also the commodity most used in trade.

Soon his family would be moving into their field hut so they could work in the paddies from dawn until dusk. Sowing the seed and transplanting the rice was strenuous work, but everyone had a good time laboring side by side. They also looked forward to harvesting the fish trapped in the deep wells in certain fields.

One night a village nearby was attacked by rebel soldiers, and the men of Ban Dao gathered at the headman's house to discuss the news. Several young men had been captured during the attack, including Song, who had worked for the missionaries. Often such captives were taken to the far north and forced to fight for the Pathet Lao rebels. The Taway people had no interest in the warring factions that were tearing the country apart, but the rebels and their political front, the *Neo Lao Hak Sat*[1], pressured everyone to become involved.

Peng's heart ached for his friend. They had visited one another several times since John and Dorothy had left, and the Christian fellowship had helped him greatly. He could imagine how frightened and lonesome his friend must feel, far from home among enemies. He often mentioned Song in his prayers after that, asking for God's protection and deliverance. It was difficult being the only Christian in Ban Dao, but at least he was safe in his own village. He didn't understand why the Laotians kept fighting one another. It seemed that peace would never return to the land.

The rains stopped, and in mid-May the fields were still not soaked enough for the rice seed to be planted. So several of the younger men decided to attend the rocket festival in town, and Peng and

---

[1] Literally, "love the race." This faction wanted to free Laos from all Western influence and align it with North Vietnam.

Lam went along. The normally quiet streets of Mong were thronged with crowds when they arrived.

Many Buddhist temples in surrounding villages had made a rocket to enter in the contest. Men playing cymbals, drums and gongs escorted the groups bringing the rockets into town. People were singing and dancing in the streets, boasting how far their rockets would shoot, doing anything to make noise and attract attention. Young men wearing colorful disguises prowled about, their faces decorated with bright streaks of makeup.

A delicate flute-like melody drifted over the scene as the *khene*[2] players entertained the people. Peng noticed that the tall flame trees were in full bloom. Stretching upward toward the clear blue sky, the vivid red blossoms danced gaily in the breeze, seeming to join in the celebration of fertility.

The men from Ban Dao wandered through the crowds, enjoying the excitement. Finally they stopped in front of a shop and squatted down to rest while waiting for the contest to begin. After a while Peng got up and walked to the marketplace. He looked at the house on the corner where John and Dorothy had lived, seeing that it was obviously empty, the doors and windows tightly closed. He talked to a shopkeeper nearby and learned the house was still unoccupied.

Peng couldn't even imagine what it was like in America; he had never been outside his own

---

[2] A flute-like musical instrument made of several lengths of bamboo.

country. He wondered if he would ever see the missionaries again. Walking back through the crowds he felt very much alone. He had nothing in common with the people about him; he didn't even understand the Laotian language very well. Now he was an outsider among his own tribe since he had become a Christian. What if the foreigners never came back? How long could he go on by himself trying to follow the true God?

He rejoined his friends and squatted down next to Lam. Feeling desolate, he barely glanced at the group of Laotian girls standing nearby, dressed in their best silk skirts and colorful shoulder scarves handwoven with gold and silver threads. Each girl wore her black hair pulled back into a smooth bun which gleamed in the bright sunlight. Most of the Taway men watched the girls shyly, but Peng stared at the crowd, seeing nothing.

A group of men with homemade puppets stopped to entertain the bystanders. Everyone laughed as two puppets boxed one another and shouted insults, and finally Peng began to smile and feel a bit more cheerful. The puppeteers made lewd jokes, but no one blushed. This was a time to relax and enjoy oneself without restraint. In a few weeks everyone would be working from dawn to dusk plowing the paddy fields and seeding them with rice, but today no one except Peng seemed to feel the cares of life.

Gradually the merrymaking subsided as the people saw a procession forming in the center of town. Several orange-robed Buddhist priests with

shaven heads seated themselves in gilded palanquins fitted with cushions. Behind them in less
ornate litters sat five sober young men who were
to become monks that day. Shaded by large
Chinese paper umbrellas, the men were absorbed
in meditation, their faces expressionless.

A gong rang out and the village men eagerly
took their places at the shafts and lifted the litters
to their shoulders, considering it an offering to
Buddha to carry his servants. Led by other monks
on foot at a slow pace the procession circled the
temple three times, followed by a crowd of men,
women and children carrying cups filled with
water and flowers. A few young men set off bursts
of firecrackers in the rear.

Finally the palanquins were lowered at an
improvised chapel made of bamboo and straw.
The men gravely dismounted and entered the
chapel, kneeling in the center before a row of
hollow bamboo tubes. The head of the diocese
and the abbots in their saffron-colored robes
poured cups of scented water into each tube. The
lustral water trickled through the tubes and fell
onto the shaven heads of the kneeling young men.
Parents, friends, and neighbors in turn poured
their cups of shimmering water into the tubes,
baptizing the newly-ordained monks and sym-
bolizing their purification. Each novice then
exchanged his damp outer robe for a new saffron-
colored one, took the fan and the pilgrim's staff
that were handed to him, and followed the abbot
out of the enclosure. Slowly they passed a row of

kneeling women who placed flowers, candles, and joss-sticks on their fans as the young men held them out.

When the monks finally disappeared into the Buddhist temple the solemn hush lifted from the crowd, and excitement returned. Housewives hurriedly served the midday meal in the long sheds that had been erected for the occasion. The Taway men were welcomed by a shopkeeper they knew and ate heartily with the others. The small fee asked for the food would be donated to the support of the temple.

Soon the entire town gathered at the riverbank near an ancient tree which leaned naturally over the water. A primitive ladder was tied onto the tree trunk, and the spectators waited impatiently as young men carefully lifted the first rocket up to the launching site. The powder and firing bore were carefully checked and when the rocket was finally in place at the very top of the tree, the long hanging fuse was lit.

The restless crowd grew silent as they watched the missile quiver and then roar, shooting up into the air and out across the river. Everyone cheered loudly, and the monk who had fashioned the rocket smiled proudly at his friends. Firing these rockets at the sky was supposed to bring good rains for the crops.

Another group of villagers brought their entry and carefully launched it in a similar way. Although beautifully decorated and nearly twenty feet long, this rocket disappointed everyone by splattering and backfiring. As it shot downward toward the ground, people jumped out of the way, booing good-naturedly and shouting ridicule at the villagers who had sponsored it.

Peng and his friends cheered and laughed with the rest of the crowd as each rocket was launched. Late that afternoon they returned home still full of excitement from the festival. Joking and feeling free from the cares of life, they gathered at Lam's house to celebrate. Peng was so grateful to be with his friends again that he joined in drinking the rice wine, but he soon became uneasy and slipped away unnoticed.

Very little rain fell that week, and the rice planting had to be delayed. Several people became ill from the extreme heat. One man had a serious accident with his machete, cutting off several fingers. The village elders consulted Samat and the other spirit priests to try to discover the cause of these troubles. Elaborate ceremonies were performed, and when the priests came out of their trance they agreed they had seen a certain angry spirit dwelling in the new granary Samat had built beside his field house.

When Samat discussed the problem with his family, Peng admitted that he had gone there many times to pray because there was no privacy at home. Someone was sure to laugh and interrupt him whenever he bowed his head to pray in his parents' one-roomed house. Although he was not ashamed to talk to Jesus in front of others, his spirit felt constrained and uneasy among curious onlookers, so he had gone into the granary where he could be completely alone.

Samat was quite upset and demanded that Peng take the responsibility for appeasing the angry spirit. Faced with such an ultimatum and the pressure of the entire village, Peng sacrificed a baby pig to satisfy the spirit's demands and encourage it to move back into the forest. However, instead of using the magic words his father had taught him, he silently prayed in the name of Jesus.

Everyone then gathered to celebrate by drinking rice wine all night, insisting that Peng join in the festivities. Seeking release from his anxieties and loneliness, he drank more than he intended.

He awoke the next morning with a severe headache. Feeling ill, he crawled out onto the porch for some fresh air. When he recalled the events of the previous day, he felt disgusted with himself. Instinctively he knew that as a follower of Jesus he had done wrong in trying to appease the spirits. He remembered he had said foolish, crude things during the night after drinking the rice wine, and he was ashamed.

He didn't want to face his friends or family so he walked slowly down to the garden house near the river where his uncle Vahn lived. For nearly a week he stayed there, sleeping most of the time until he felt better. He refused to eat for several days, even though he became weak and his eyesight seemed blurred. Vahn left him alone when he saw he didn't want to talk.

Peng wondered if he could go on being a Christian. Would God forgive him for his failure? It was so difficult being the only believer. He knew he was not strong enough always to do the right thing.

He sat on the porch for hours trying to remember what the missionary had taught him. Finally he prayed, "Oh, God in heaven, if it is Your will that You would lead me and help me, I will never drink rice wine again." Then within his heart he seemed to hear a voice saying, *From now on I will make you strong.*

Strength began to flow back into him as he sensed God's love and forgiveness. But he still refused to eat, spending the next two days in prayer, thanking God for His love. As his spirit grew stronger, God's presence became very real. He realized that power to resist sin came through prayer and that only by close fellowship with the true God would he find the strength to stand.

At last the heavy monsoon rains came. Suk had soaked the seed thoroughly in large pots while the fields were being flooded and plowed. Peng and his father took turns walking through the mud to guide the wooden plow as it was pulled by a water buffalo. Every other day Samat let one buffalo rest and hitched up his other one for plowing.

Then the water was let out of the dikes, and the rice was sowed in the sticky mud. Several days later when the seed had sprouted, the drains in the dikes were again blocked so the rains could gradually flood the fields. At last everyone could rest for a few days as they waited for the seedlings to grow tall enough to be transplanted and spaced out properly in the other fields.

Peng and his parents always moved down into the field house at this time of the year so they could keep watch over the young rice and protect it from birds and other dangers during the daytime. This house was much smaller than their mountain home, so Peng again needed a private place for prayer, and he decided to use an old granary on the edge of the fields. The first day he went there for prayer he committed the building to God and in Jesus' name commanded all evil spirits to leave. He had learned an important lesson from his bad experience with the spirit that lived in his father's new granary. If he ignored the demons they would cause much trouble, but if he took the offensive in the power of Jesus, the spirits had to leave.

Inside the small bamboo hut two bins made of large woven mats were filled with rice, braced on the sides by wooden planks. There was just enough room in front of the storage bins for him to sit with his legs stretched out comfortably. He could shut the sliding bamboo door, and no one would know he was there. Since the ventilation was inadequate, he often felt hot and sticky on humid days, but it was a small price to pay for the blessing of being alone with God.

About two months after the rainy season began, he heard the rumor that a foreigner was again living in Mong, not in the house where John and Dorothy had lived but across the river on the south bank. He hurried into town as soon as he could, and a shopkeeper directed him to an Englishman named Don Wilson, who said he was a friend of John's. Don's own mission station farther north had been overrun by rebel troops, and as he was unable to return there, he had been asked to fill the need in Mong temporarily.

Peng's spirit revived as Don read God's Word to him, but then he became convicted of sin. He told Don he had made a sacrifice to the spirits and had gotten drunk. "Is God angry with me?" he asked.

Don said, "If you enjoyed doing things like that, it would show you had not really become a child of God. But because you realize it is wrong and have now repented, I'm sure you are a Christian. God is not angry. He loves you very much and will always forgive you when you confess your sins."

"Why do I have so many troubles and temptations?" Peng asked. "Am I a greater sinner than other people? Others seem to have an easy life, but I always have problems."

"Everyone has sinned," Don answered. "Even those who appear happy and prosperous are sinners in God's sight." He opened his Bible to Romans, chapter three, and pointed to verse 23. "For all have sinned and come short of the glory of God," he read.

Peng took the Bible and read the words for himself. He read them a second and third time but still didn't understand. Could it be that rich people were sinners just as much as poor people? He had always heard that troubles and poverty came to men in proportion to their sins.

Reading the verse again, Peng realized it meant there were *no* good and righteous people on the earth. Not even religious people were accepted in God's sight.

He read the verse a fifth and sixth time. Then he realized the main point was that he himself hadn't lived up to the righteous standard of God. Yet God had found him and saved him, and would surely keep him, no matter what troubles he experienced.

Don gave him several new Lao tracts to take home, as well as a small booklet containing the Gospel of Mark from God's Word. Peng decided it was wrong to hide these from his family as though he were ashamed of them, so he read a tract openly that evening before the sun went down.

Samat frowned when he saw Peng reading the paper with Laotian writing on it. "Where did you get that?" he asked.

"A foreigner in town gave it to me," Peng answered cautiously.

Samat grunted and stared at his son. Where had he learned to read? Why couldn't he be contented with the traditions of their own people? Yet he felt strangely proud that Peng was ambitious and clever enough to read the odd-looking marks on the paper.

"Don't read out loud. I don't want to hear

the foreigner's words," he said. But he didn't forbid Peng to read, since they were living in the field house. Peng knew he wouldn't be allowed to take any books up into the mountain village.

Several weeks later Peng was alone in the field house reading. The book of Mark fascinated him, as it described the miracles and teachings of Jesus. The words in this book seemed to satisfy his craving to know God more intimately. He pronounced the words softly, struggling with some of the difficult Laotian syllables, trying to grasp the meaning. Since a high or low tone changed the meaning of a word, it was easier to read out loud than to try to say the words inside his head.

A shadow fell across the doorway. Startled, he looked up and saw Heng staring at him. "So that's what you do when you are alone," Heng said. "You are reading a Laotian book!"

"Yes," said Peng, his eyes flashing, as his heart constricted in fear. Heng would be sure to tell others. He realized his secret would soon be known all over the village, but he resolved to remain calm and not show his concern.

"Come in and sit down," he invited. He had been wanting an opportunity to talk to Heng. If only they could be friends again!

But Heng refused to enter the house. "You think you're the smartest one in the village, don't you!" he accused. "But you didn't get Lansee for a wife, did you? And now you want to introduce foreign ways into Ban Dao. Wait until the spirit priests hear what you are doing!" He turned and left before Peng could answer.

Kept By the Power of God

9

Kept By the Power of God

HENG REPORTED HIS discovery to the headman and elders of Ban Dao, and later that week the entire village was called together for a meeting in a large open space near the headman's house. Even the women and children were present. The rain had ceased temporarily, and the sun shone weakly through the scattered clouds that scudded across the sky. The ground was nearly dry. Everyone was glad to see some sunshine, but an uncomfortable humidity permeated the air, adding to Peng's tension.

Sitting above the crowd on his verandah, the headman raised his right hand, signalling that he was ready to begin the meeting. "Peng, son of Samat, has offended the spirits," he declared as the villagers waited in silence, looking up at him expectantly. "First he decided to follow the foreigner's God, and now he is bringing Laotian books into our village." A murmur of surprise and disapproval rose from the assembly.

Heng stood and Tuat motioned for him to speak. "Samat's younger son Khap has gone to live in Solane and is working for the Laotians. Samat and his family are not loyal to the ways of our ancestors."

Kambit and the other spirit priests sitting near Peng's father looked at him with disfavor. Several of them were already jealous of his popularity, so they eagerly welcomed this opportunity to discredit him through his family. Withdrawing from him, they conferred together quietly.

Shocked at the accusation, Samat stood up immediately to defend his sons. His thick black hair seemed to bristle more than usual. Though dressed only in the traditional black-and-white plaid Taway loincloth, his tall well-built frame radiated dignity and strength.

"My sons have broken no tribal laws," he said. "When their curiosity is satisfied, they will return to the ways of our people. We don't live in bondage to one another. Young people need to be free to make their own choices, as long as they are careful not to offend the spirits."

Samat argued eloquently for several minutes and then concluded, "Peng has not brought any Laotian books up into the main village. We allow bicycles to be kept in our field houses, so books should be allowed, too. It's not good to be ignorant of the ways of the Laotians and the foreigners, lest they get an advantage over us. If the spirits are offended, they will reveal it." Although Samat was somewhat apprehensive that his sons' actions would antagonize the spirits, he loved Peng and Khap and he was determined to protect them.

Samat was a clever speaker and had much good sense. Several men stood and called out comments to show their agreement with him, for he had helped many people in their time of need, and had many loyal friends.

Then Tuat motioned for Peng to speak. As he stood up the sky darkened suddenly. Thick grey clouds blocked the sun, and a brisk wind swept over the crowd. Peng felt as if he was surrounded by the powers of darkness, but he spoke boldly. "I love our Taway people, and I don't want to bring trouble to anyone. I've found that walking in the Jesus path brings peace and joy. My books tell about the true God who created the sun and the earth, the one who has supreme power over all the demons who oppress us. I want to read these books that tell of Him, so I can show all of you the upward path to true happiness, but I will not take the books into the main village or do anything that would bring trouble to our people."

Several others gave their opinions and then the spirit priests consulted quietly, excluding Samat from their midst. Finally Kambit, a powerful *shaman* in the village, gave the verdict.

"No fine will be imposed this time," he said. "But we must watch Peng carefully and see that he doesn't violate our traditions. No Laotian books will be allowed into the mountain village." A murmur of approval swept through the Taway assembly, which quickly broke up and scattered as a light rain began falling. Unsatisfied, Heng stood glaring at Peng angrily and then turned on his heel and left in silence. Samat watched him go, aware that they had an enemy who would not easily give up.

The family was very quiet when they gathered for supper that evening. A steady rain was now falling, with intermittent flashes of lightning and claps of thunder. It felt good to be safe and warm inside the little bamboo field house.

Peng mumbled a word of thanks to his father for his support that afternoon. Samat gave him a stern look, saying, "Next time you will have to defend yourself, but they have no right to accuse our family of disloyalty. We are loyal Taway."

Suddenly the wind howled and blew fistfuls of rain through the partially open doorway. Peng jumped up to slide a woven partition firmly across the entrance. Thunder growled overhead as if a huge beast were roaming across the sky. Jesus created the rain and He controls all storms, Peng told himself as he settled back down to finish his meal. Maybe God is trying to tell the village He is on my side! Thunder and lightning used to frighten him sometimes, but not since he had put his trust in Jesus.

When everyone had finished eating, Samat sighed, glancing at Peng. "You should put aside these strange ideas of yours. The foreigners have forgotten all about you and will not be coming back."

Out of respect for his father Peng repressed a heated retort. He felt the missionaries cared about him almost more than his own tribe did, but he said nothing, sure that John and Dorothy would return someday. If his father tried to prevent him from following the Jesus way, maybe he would leave home like his brother. His jaw clenched stubbornly. He was not going to be pushed around!

It rained nearly every day for several weeks as the monsoon season continued. At last the rice seedlings were transplanted and seemed to be growing well. Peng's parents moved back into the mountain village, leaving him in charge of the field work, although they often came down to help. He kept busy repairing the dikes which sometimes broke after a heavy downpour. He also had to watch carefully that crabs didn't crawl over the dikes and destroy the young rice plants. He longed to go into town to see if anyone had come to live in the mission house, but travel was slow and difficult during the rainy season. He knew that the unpaved motor road would be a mass of slippery mud.

★   ★   ★   ★

Lam hurried through Ban Dao late one sunny afternoon in mid August. He had just returned from town and was eager to get home for supper, but first he wanted to tell Peng the news. So instead of following the rocky path around a pile of boulders, he took a short cut across the muddy hillside. When he reached Peng's house he saw Ying on the porch.

"Is Peng home?" he called.

"No, he's still working in the fields," she answered. "But he's coming up to the village for supper tonight."

Lam stood still, feeling disappointed. He hadn't crossed the rice fields, having come home a different way through the forest. He looked up at Ying. "Tell him I'll come over after I eat. I have some news from Mong."

When Lam returned later that evening Peng was waiting for him on the verandah in the fading light. "Come on up," he called. "I hear you have news for me."

Lam scrambled up the pole ladder, excitement evident on his face. "Some foreigners are living in the mission house in Mong!" he said. "I talked with them today."

"Come inside and tell me about them," Peng invited. They sat down together on the mat beside the firebed where the evening meal had been cooked. A few bright coals still gleamed in the ashes, and a burning pine chip threw a flickering light across the room onto the faces of Peng's parents who sat quietly near the small window chewing betel nut. Ying gathered the enamel plates used for supper and went outside to rinse them off on the verandah.

"Three white women are living in the mission home now," Lam reported.

"Women!" Peng exclaimed. He didn't want to talk to foreign women. How could women teach him anything? "Where are their husbands? Surely they didn't come without their husbands!" he said.

"None of them mentioned having a family," Lam replied. "I didn't see any children, and I don't think any men are living there. But they knew about you and are hoping you will visit them soon."

"They must be friends of *Than* John and his wife," Peng said hesitantly. Perhaps their husbands were away on a trip and would return soon.

"They're brave to stay in Mong without husbands." Samat spoke softly from the shadows. "I heard that last week Vietminh troops came close to the town from the east before the Laotian soldiers drove them away."

"Did the women tell you about Jesus?" Peng looked at his friend hopefully. Perhaps Lam would become a Christian now that some missionaries were in town and could teach him.

"Yes, they told me the same things you've been saying." Lam glanced apprehensively at Samat. "But I can't leave the way of the spirits."

Peng wanted to hurry into town the next morning to meet the new missionaries, but it rained hard for several days. When the weather cleared there was so much to do in the fields that his father came down to help him. They spent hours together weeding the fields with a hoe and repairing dikes which had been weakened by the heavy rains.

Anger and resentment smouldered inside Peng. He was on the verge of demanding that he be allowed some free time to go into town, but then some verses he read in Mark changed his mind.[1]

---

[1] Mark 8:34-35 and 10:43-45

They said that Jesus served others and expected His followers to do the same, denying themselves. So he continued to work quietly beside his father.

One day Samat grumbled, "Khap should be here to help his family, not off in town taking wages from strangers." Country people in Laos felt that anyone who would stoop to hiring himself out to work for others was an inferior person, practically a slave.

Peng nodded. "I wish Khap would come back home." He felt his jealousy and resentment return. He couldn't take even one day off to go visit the missionaries, but Khap was free to go wherever he wanted. He knew it was best that families stick together and help one another, yet he wished he were independent like his brother. However, he loved his father and longed to lead him to Christ, so he suffered in silence and worked diligently, asking Jesus to make him more patient and unselfish.

Every day Samat seemed to invent new jobs. They had many large fields to care for, and although Suk and Ying were also coming down to help as they always did at this busy time of the year, with Khap away in Solane everyone had to work longer hours than usual. Often they kept working even when it rained.

One morning Peng noticed the sky clearing. Perhaps today there would be no rain! "I wish I could go into town today," he mumbled, unable to keep quiet any longer.

Suk heard him and glanced questioningly

at her husband, but Samat seemed to pretend he hadn't heard the remark. For days now Suk had sensed Peng's carefully controlled impatience to go meet the new missionaries. She was amazed that he hadn't lashed out at his father with angry words. Her heart softened and she said quietly to Peng, "I'd like you to take some bananas into town to sell. The fruit is ripe and should bring a good price." She had noticed that Peng was more patient and kind since he started following the Jesus way. Surely it wouldn't hurt for him to visit the missionaries.

Peng looked at his father eagerly. Would he allow him to go?

Samat frowned and his lips pulled back into a thin line. He didn't want Peng to get involved with any foreigners again, especially strange women. He looked resentfully at Suk and then at his son's eager face. If he didn't allow him some freedom, Peng might leave home like his brother had. Finally he nodded in agreement.

"Yes, that's a good idea. The fruit is ready to be picked and we need the cash." He had planted the trees before Peng was born, for bananas were popular with the Laotians and provided an extra source of income for the family.

"I'll get ready and go right away," Peng said, jumping down from the low porch of the field house before Samat could say more. He hurried up to the mountain house and cut down two large branches of bananas from the trees nearby. Using strips of vine he tied a stalk to each end of his carrying pole.

The hot morning sun was burning overhead as he left the village, the pole with its heavy burden over one shoulder and his sandals, tied together with string, hanging over the other. It was more comfortable walking barefooted. In spite of the sunshine, the path was still muddy from the past weeks of rain, and Peng's feet squished pleasantly in the cool mud as he trotted along. He would wash his feet in the river when he got to town and then put on his clean sandals so he would look his best when he met the missionaries. His tattered white shirt was soon wet with sweat as the humidity rose with the temperature, but he was glad he had not waited until the next morning, even though he would have been more comfortable travelling in the early hours after dawn. Anyway, his father might have changed his mind by then, or another heavy rainstorm might have begun.

He was very hot and tired when he reached the small Laotian village of Tahin, about halfway to Mong. He walked slowly through it, looking for someone to give him a drink of water. Small bamboo houses were scattered among the more sturdy wooden homes, all built up on stilts, but not as high as the Taway built theirs. The village appeared deserted, most of the people having already left to work in their fields.

Suddenly a voice called out, "Where are you going with that fruit, young man?" Peng turned around and saw a toothless old man sitting on the porch of a small bamboo house. "I'll buy your bananas," he said, beckoning.

"I'm going to sell them in Mong," Peng replied. "But I would like a drink of water."

"Come drink all you want," the man invited. As Peng walked over to the porch two small children came out of the house, followed by a woman whose grey hair was cropped short to show she was past childbearing age. Grandparents often cared for the small children while the rest of the family was out in the fields.

"I want some bananas," she said. "I'll pay you for them."

Peng hesitated. The Laotians in this village always wanted to buy produce from the Taway at a bargain rate so they could resell it for a profit, but he was determined to get a good price for his bananas in town. Bending his knees, he lowered the carrying pole and set the load of fruit carefully on the ground.

"I'll sell you twelve bananas for ten *kip*, grand-mother," he finally said. He broke off a large hand of bananas from one stalk and handed them to the old woman. She gave him a dipper full of water, and as he drank she went back into the house and came out with some money. Taking the handful of cash, he counted the grubby wrinkled bills. There were only five.

"Only five *kip*? That's not a fair price!" he exclaimed. He knew he could get twice that amount in town . . . but these people had given him water to drink. He decided not to argue.

After a second drink of water he thanked the man and his wife, hoisted the load of bananas and his sandals onto his shoulders, and strode back to the road.

He arrived in Mong two hours later and sold the fruit for a good price to his shopkeeper friend. He was hungry, but of course the market had already closed. Later he might go eat at a restaurant, but first he wanted to visit the missionaries.

Quickly he went down to the riverside and washed his feet, letting them dry in the sunshine before putting on his sandals. He was beginning to feel nervous. When he reached the mission house he peered through the open front door. No one was there, but he heard voices in the adjoining room. Too shy to call out a greeting, he went around to the side door. It was cut in two, and the top half was open. He took a deep breath, walked up to the door, and looked inside. He saw a tall young woman with curly hair working in the kitchen. He coughed gently to announce his presence, and she looked up, her face hot and flushed from cooking over a charcoal brazier.

"*Sambai baw*! I'm Peng from Ban Dao," he said.

"Oh, you've come at last!" the woman exclaimed. "Peng is here," she called out to her friends. Two other white women came hurrying to meet him. Smiling and nodding happily, they invited him inside, and they all sat down to get acquainted.

"John and Dorothy told us you trusted in Jesus before they left here last spring. We've been so eager to meet you, Peng. My name is Anna," said the woman with dark hair pulled back into a smooth bun like Lao women combed their hair. She wore a white blouse and a brightly colored wrap-around Lao skirt. "This is Ursula, and this is Rosemary," she said, introducing the other women. Peng couldn't pronounce their strange foreign names, so they worked out a simpler form that he could say and remember easily.

He noticed that they all wore rubber thong sandals like the ones he himself was wearing. He was glad he had on the ones he had bought in town, not those made from old truck tires. It seemed strange to wear them inside the house, but like the Chinese and Vietnamese shopkeepers and the Filipino doctor at the clinic, these foreigners seemed to wear their sandals all the time.

"Where are your husbands?" Peng asked.

"Oh, we're not married," Rosemary said. "But Ursula will be getting married next year. Her young man is living in Solane now." The short woman with light brown hair smiled shyly at Peng.

Anna explained, "Rosemary and I haven't found the right man yet, but we don't mind being single. God takes care of us."

"I'm not married, either," Peng said slowly, wondering if he should talk so freely to these women. Did they really care about him? Or would they become bored with him and ignore him the next time he came to visit? Since being rejected by Lansee he didn't trust any woman very much. "Sometimes it's hard being unmarried, but I still live with my parents," he added cautiously. "Who is taking care of your parents while you are here in this country?"

"They aren't very old yet and don't really need us," Ursula said. "They were happy for us to bring God's Word to Laos."

Astounded, Peng sat speechlessly staring at the three women. How could any parents let their unmarried daughters travel to a foreign land? It was incomprehensible! But maybe believing in Jesus caused people to overcome their natural fears, he decided. These women must feel that it was very important to bring God's message to Laos.

"Aren't there enough men willing to come preach in Laos?" he asked finally.

"No," the women answered in unison, shaking their heads sadly. Rosemary added, "I'm just glad that God can use women as well as men. It's wonderful to have a part in doing His work here in Laos."

Peng thought about that for a moment, but he remained puzzled. Perhaps foreign men were very lazy and let women do their work!

"I came to learn more from God's book," he said finally.

They invited him to sit with them at a table nearby, and each woman opened a large heavy book. Anna explained that this was the Laotian Bible, God's words translated into the Laotian language. She put her copy in front of Peng and indicated a verse with her finger. He followed the words as the curly-headed woman read, "A sower went out to sow."

After each woman had read a few lines, Anna invited Peng to read. Stumblingly he read a few words. Many of the words he had never seen before, and he was uncertain of their meaning. The print in this book was smaller and more difficult to read than in the book of Mark that *Than* Don had given him.

Rosemary explained the meaning of the story. "The seed is the Word of God. He wants His words spread all over the world. That's why we came here to live. Many of the Laotian people have hearts like the hard soil; they are interested only in earning merit according to the teachings of Buddha. They don't seem to want the gift of righteousness that Jesus offers them, and the seed cannot get into their hearts. But other people, like yourself, have hearts like good soil and they receive the truth."

Peng asked many questions, and the women discussed the Bible verses until they were sure he understood. They often turned to other verses in the Bible to explain a point, and he realized they must have studied God's words for many years to know so much about them.

When Rosemary went to prepare some food to eat, Anna opened her Bible to the Gospel of John. Peng listened intently as she read from the first chapter, explaining that Jesus had created all things in the beginning. His eyes shone with satisfaction as he said, "I knew the evil spirits couldn't have made the sun and stars and the earth. I thought a Good Spirit must have made them, and I was determined to find Him."

Soon freshly-steamed rice and a Laotian stew were placed on the table, and he was invited to share the meal. He ate hesitantly at first, but then ravenously, surprised that the foreign women could cook such tasty food. They talked happily as they ate together, and suddenly Peng realized that it didn't seem strange at all to be eating with these women, although he hardly ever ate with women at home. The missionaries' single-minded love for Jesus and their interest in him made him feel very relaxed and secure. It seemed as if they were all part of the same family, although he had known them only a few hours. He was also impressed that they spoke Laotian so well. He resolved that he would study hard until he, too, could speak it fluently, even though he naturally preferred his own language.

As they ate he told the women how difficult and lonely it was to be the only Christian in his village. "We know it's not easy," Anna agreed. "We pray for you every day that you will be strong to stand for Jesus, and that you will keep away from all forms of demon worship. I can see that already God has taught you many things."

After the meal Peng was eager to study again. Rosemary gave him a large Laotian Bible with a dark red cover. She underlined several verses with a bright red pencil so he could find them again easily and study them at home.

He especially liked the words of 1 Peter 1:5, "Who are kept by the power of God through faith for a salvation ready to be revealed in the last time." It was comforting to know that God was keeping him safe, helping him not to fall back into the old life.

God's book said that the trial of his faith was much more precious than gold. The missionary teacher seemed to understand that being a Christian wasn't easy for him. She told him it would be worth all the suffering when he saw Jesus face to face in heaven someday.

She talked to him for nearly an hour, but Peng didn't feel tired. He sat motionless, his eyes fixed in total concentration on her face, his mouth hanging open. He was unaware of time passing or of the heat of the afternoon. When Rosemary's voice grew tired, Anna came to teach him, and then Ursula took a turn. Still his eagerness to learn was unquenched.

"I'd better leave now," he said finally, realizing that it was late in the afternoon. "I need to get home before dark." He put his carrying pole over his shoulder and picked up the Bible they had given him.

"We have a church meeting here tomorrow and every Sunday," Anna told him. "Come and worship the Lord Jesus with us whenever you can."

When Peng reached the edge of town he took his shirt off and wrapped the heavy Lao Bible in it, tying the sleeves together to make a handle so he

KEPT BY THE POWER OF GOD   115

could carry the bundle more easily. He wanted to protect the beautiful book of God and keep it as clean as possible.

Maybe now my father will be willing to listen to God's words, he thought, as he hurried along the road toward the setting sun. When Khap comes home from Solane I'll tell him about Jesus, too!

He pushed to the back of his mind the ugly fear that the village priests might take the book of God away from him or accuse him of causing trouble in Ban Dao if he continued to talk about Jesus.

10

Taught By the Spirit

PENG CONTINUED LIVING in the field house alone.
He liked the privacy and freedom he had there
to study his Bible when he wasn't busy repairing
the dikes or weeding. He spent many hours
puzzling over the words the missionary women
had marked in red in the big Laotian Bible they
had given him.

One verse was very easy to understand and it
became his favorite. "For God loved mankind all
over the world so very much, even to the extent
that He gave them His Son, the only Son He had,
that each person who believes in the Son shall not
perish, but shall have the life that goes on and on
forever."[1]

That verse seemed to summarize the message of
Jesus very clearly, so he read it eagerly to anyone
who would listen. The village leaders watched him
closely, but could do nothing as long as he kept his
books outside the village. Soon a group of children
began to come by the field hut in the afternoons to
hear stories about Jesus. Their curiosity was
stronger than their fear of the spirit priests' threats.

Sometimes Lam came as well, anxious to
discover why God's book was so important to

---
[1] John 3:16

Peng. He found there were no magic words, just simple stories of man's sin and God's love. When there were difficult words he would help Peng pronounce the strange syllables, although he often had no idea of their meaning.

Unperturbed, Peng would read the verses over and over, then close his eyes and pray, "Oh, God, show me the meaning of these words. Help me understand what you are saying to me." Then he would read the verses again and meditate on them silently until an idea came to him, which he would share with his audience.

"He who believes in the Son will have life that lasts forever," Peng read to Lam one day, "but he who does not believe in the Son shall not see life, but the wrath of God hangs over him."[2]

Lam's heart constricted with fear as he listened. He didn't like the idea that God was angry with him. Peng's God was obviously very powerful; He had kept him safe from the evil spirits many months now. Perhaps it would be wise to start following Jesus, Lam decided.

A few days later he had an errand in town, and after it was done he spent several hours with the missionaries, asking questions and listening to verses from God's book. The Jesus way seemed to be a path of peace and happiness, and Lam longed to have the joy and courage he had seen in Peng. It would be wonderful to have the protection of this God and never again be afraid of the evil

---

[2] John 3:36

spirits or of death. But part of him held back. His wife would ridicule him and be angry if he were to begin following the foreign God. His relatives would accuse him of being disloyal to the tribal spirits, and he would be blamed for any bad luck that happened to his family. He decided sadly that he would have to think about the decision for a while longer.

"The Jesus way is good," he finally told the missionaries. "But I'm not sure I can follow Him now, because it would make my family angry with me. I must think about this more carefully before I make a decision."

The rains were not so frequent now, and there was less to do in the rice fields. Peng took most of the responsibility for repairing the paddy dikes and keeping the pigs and other animals out of the fields, and sometimes his father would come down from the mountain village early in the morning to help him. When the sun was hot but not yet straight above them, they would stop to eat the first meal of the day.

"Come up to the village and eat with us today," Samat invited one morning. "You haven't visited us for a long time." Lately Peng had been cooking his own meals and eating alone at the field house.

Suk was setting the plates out on the bamboo mat beside the fire when Peng and his father came through the doorway wiping the sweat from their faces.

"Hurry, mother, I'm about to die of hunger," Peng said jokingly. Suk smiled. She set the steaming pot over near the edge of the firebed on some cool ashes, took out a spoonful of rice, and carried it to a small shelf built high on one wall. Mumbling a few words, she put the rice onto a tiny bamboo plate on the shelf beside a handful of chicken feathers covered with dried blood.

Peng had seen his mother perform this ceremony hundreds of times, but now he stared as if he had never seen it before. It was so automatic to pay respect to one's ancestors that he hadn't thought much about it. He knew the Chinese and the Laotians had similar customs honoring their ancestors. The Taway women in each family usually took care of this obligation, representing the rest of the family.

Now Peng suddenly realized this was an act of worship, done not only in respect but also in fear that punishment would follow if the ritual was not observed. Because of the token offering, the meal sitting before him was now dedicated to the spirits of his ancestors. He no longer feared them as his parents did, but by eating the food he would be sharing in ancestor worship.

"I'm not hungry," he blurted out. Suk's mouth dropped open, and Samat frowned. "I mean I can't eat this rice," Peng explained. "It's been offered to the ancestor spirits, and I don't believe we should worship them or try to appease them."

"Sickness and trouble come to those who

don't honor their ancestors," Samat warned. "This is our Taway tradition."

"I remember my grandparents with love in my heart," Peng assured his father, "but I don't believe it is necessary to appease them with offerings. Wherever our ancestors are now, they still love us and wouldn't harm us," he insisted.

Samat and Suk were angry and hurt when Peng returned to the field house without eating with them. For nearly a week they didn't go down to the fields to see him.

Peng himself felt shocked that he had been involved in spirit worship these many months since becoming a Christian. "Please forgive me," he prayed to God. "I didn't realize I was disobeying your words. Thank you for showing me I was doing wrong."

He suddenly remembered that the missionaries had showed him a verse about being forgiven for sin, and carefully searched through the places marked in red in his Bible. Finally he found the words near the end of the book.

"If we admit our sins, God is faithful and righteous to forgive our sins, and He will wash us from all unrighteousness."[3] He marveled at God's goodness. God had not sent illness to punish him for doing wrong, but had been patient with him and helped him realize his error.

Suk couldn't understand Peng's actions, but she had seen his determination and she knew he

[3] 1 John 1:9

wouldn't waver. He always kept his temper under control now and was gentle and kind, patient with everyone. Although she couldn't put it into words, her love and admiration for her son were growing. She missed him, and she could see that Samat also longed to see his son again.

Finally she discussed the matter with her husband, who eventually relented and sent Ying to the field house with a message for Peng.

"Mother and father want you to come eat with us tomorrow," she told him. "Mother says that from now on she will always dish up your food before she makes the offering to the ancestors."

Peng was relieved that his parents wanted to see him again. He realized he must be patient with them, for they didn't understand his new way of life. He ate at the mountain house frequently after that and was careful to show love and respect toward his parents in every way he could.

Soon after this, the village young people began talking about the school festival which was to be held in Mong shortly. All the tribes had been invited to send a delegation, but although other tribes usually went, the Taway rarely did, for they knew that if their young people saw the games and good times the Laotian children had, they might beg to attend school.

This year officials from Solane and Saravene were coming, and the ceremonies were to be held on Sunday morning. Peng heard that Lam was going with some other friends, but he hadn't been invited to go along. Lately he had noticed that some of the other young men in the village were refusing to speak to him because of his new religion.

Although his parents didn't know it, he had been to a school fair one time several years ago. The celebration was not like a religious *boun*[4] held at the temple. It was only a formal demonstration of the social and athletic progress of the province. School children, soldiers, and tribal people came dressed in their best clothes, and lined up in neat rows forming a rectangle around the speaker's booth which was made of palm branch arches.

It had rained the time Peng was there, but the people had stood at attention patiently in the light drizzle as the army colonel had led the governor around to inspect them. Then they had remained standing in the rain as the governor made a speech over the loudspeaker.

Finally everyone had been allowed to relax and find a comfortable place to watch from as the school children entertained the crowd with relays and races. In one contest each child in a certain age group had to take a mouthful of water from a basin and then run to put it into a jar to see who could fill his jar first. The audience had laughed and shouted encouragement, but only one child had lost a mouthful of water in the excitement.

---

[4] Literally, "merit". Several times each year *bouns* are held all over Laos, not only for entertainment, but also so people can earn merit for their next life.

Then some boys were blindfolded, given long heavy sticks, and led to a row of earthen jars suspended from a pole. One boy broke a jar on his third try, freeing a live chicken which had been imprisoned inside.

It had been fun to watch the games and join in the laughter, and Peng thought he would enjoy going again; but not if he was alone. Anyway, it was to be on a Sunday, and he decided he would rather study with the missionaries then. But he did feel hurt that his friends had ignored him, since this was something not connected with spirit worship, and he would have enjoyed being with them.

The very next day Lam came out to the field hut to see him. "Would you like to go to the festival with us on Sunday?" he asked. "We don't need to tell anyone where we're going. It'll be lots of fun to watch the games."

11
Witnessing

BEFORE DAWN THE next Sunday Peng walked across the fields to the forest path where he was to meet his friends. He reviewed his plans for the day. After the opening ceremonies and games were over he would invite the fellows to visit the missionaries with him. Away from the influence of the village elders, perhaps they would be curious enough to go and listen to the Gospel. Even if they refused, he himself would go to see the women teachers again. He hadn't been back since his first visit a few weeks ago, and there was so much he wanted to learn.

The faint streaks of dawn in the eastern sky steadily grew brighter as Peng waited beside the trail, under the large oak tree which the young people of his village had long used as a meeting place. His friends were late. Lam had said they would gather at dawn, and he had been there well before that time. Finally he went down to the motor road, but there was no sign of anyone walking in the distance.

Evidently the boys had left earlier or gone another way to avoid him. Peng told himself they weren't really his friends, anyway. They didn't want him around, so why should he want to be with them?

He squatted down beside the path and considered what he should do. He did want to hear the missionaries teach God's word today, but it would be very noisy with the fair going on in the marketplace right outside their front door. And perhaps he would get into trouble if he went into the mission house instead of taking his place with the tribes lined up outside to watch the ceremonies. Yet he didn't want to stand with Lam and the others if they were going to ignore him or ridicule him.

"Oh God, show me what to do," he prayed.

Finally he stood up and walked slowly back to the field house. He felt confused and humiliated. It was so lonely following the Jesus way.

When the next Saturday came Peng decided he couldn't wait any longer to visit the missionaries. Quickly he did his early morning chores in the fields and ate a few handfuls of cold rice left over from the night before, then hurried off to town. It was noontime and very hot when he reached Mong. The streets were almost deserted; nearly everyone had gone inside to escape from the noonday sun.

Anna was studying at the table in the reception room when she saw him standing shyly in the doorway. "*Sambai baw*, Peng!" she exclaimed. "I'm so glad you've come!" The other women heard them talking and soon came downstairs. They talked together all afternoon, trying to answer his questions and encourage him. "We look forward to your visits very much, Peng. Come every week if you can," Rosemary told him.

He had brought his large Bible with him so they could underline more important verses in red. "It helps me find the verses when I'm looking for them at home," he explained. Anna showed him that the Bible was divided into many smaller books and short sections called chapters, and gradually he began to understand how to locate certain verses.

Rosemary told him about a great flood which had once covered the earth, and she gave him a colored picture illustrating the story. On the back of the picture she wrote the story in simple words, also the book, chapter, and verse number where he could find it in his Bible. As he examined the picture carefully the meaning of the Bible lesson became clearer.

It no longer felt strange to be taught by the foreign women, for already they seemed like old friends. They were polite and kind, always patient when he didn't understand something. They had gentle, happy voices, and he felt at ease with them.

However, he still wondered how they could bear to live in a strange land so far away from their parents, especially without husbands. Evidently sharing God's words was more important than having a family. The Taway people allowed their women much authority in family affairs, and he gathered that foreign women were given even more freedom.

"Where did you live before you came here to Mong?" he asked Rosemary, the tall woman with the curly hair.

"My first two years I was in a town called Takong. I lived with some older, more experienced missionaries and studied the language," she explained. "We often rode our bicycles through the forest to visit with the village people and tell them about Jesus. Later I moved to another town, and while I was there a young Lao boy and a tribal man trusted in Jesus. But then the rebels moved into that area, and I had to leave very quickly. I got out just one day before the rebel army attacked and took over the town."

"Was that a large town like Mong?" Peng was very curious, for he had never traveled much and knew very little about his country.

"Oh no, it was a very small place, really just a big village. It didn't have any paved roads, and just a few shops. I don't know why they called it a *muong*,"[1] Rosemary laughed. "I guess they hoped it would grow into a large town."

"Will you go back there someday to teach those people about Jesus?" asked Peng.

"Yes, if the government regains control of that part of Laos. But at present nobody is allowed to travel to those places near the demilitarized zone

---

[1] This is the Laotian word used to indicate a town or important village.

of South Vietnam. Even if a Laotian person went to visit his relatives there, he would never be permitted to leave. But even if I can't go back and see the Christians in those places, I know I'll see them in heaven."

"Maybe the Lao rebels will attack Mong someday and capture you. Aren't you afraid to live here?"

"No, because Jesus sent me here and He has promised always to be with me. And I have many friends in America who pray every day for my safety. But if I were captured, that would be an opportunity to tell the rebel soldiers about Jesus. God will give me strength to bear whatever suffering He allows." As Rosemary spoke, the other women nodded confidently, agreeing with her.

"Tomorrow is Sunday," Anna said. "That is a special day for Christians, because Jesus rose from the dead on the first day of the week. We have a worship service every Sunday morning, and I wish you could stay to be with us tomorrow."

"You could probably sleep at our neighbor's house," said Ursula. She explained that they were a Vietnamese family who claimed to be Christians, and they often came to church. Peng agreed to stay, but he was disappointed in the Vietnamese family. They didn't read the Bible or pray before going to bed at night. They weren't very friendly either, but of course they didn't speak much Laotian.

The only ones present at the meeting the next morning were three of the Vietnamese children, the missionary women, and himself. Anna led the service, beginning it with prayer, and then everyone sang together praising Jesus. The happy songs warmed Peng's heart even though he didn't know the tune yet and couldn't understand all the words. Then there was more prayer and a lesson from God's book. Peng especially enjoyed hearing his new friends talk to God, and he joined in and prayed eagerly at every opportunity.

After dinner together Ursula and Rosemary were teaching him from John 14 when Lam appeared in the doorway. He glanced sheepishly at Peng as he sat down beside him at the table. They hadn't talked together since Lam had gone off to the school festival without him the week before. Peng smiled at his friend and decided to forgive him, thinking, perhaps today he will become a Christian!

He pushed his Bible over in front of Lam and showed him where they were studying. Ursula read the words of Jesus, "I am the Way, I am the Truth, and I am the Life. No one can come to the Father unless they come through Me."[2] After they took turns reading several verses, Rosemary explained why Jesus was the only way to heaven.

Finally she asked Lam, "Are you ready to

---

[2] John 14:6

believe in Jesus?"

He hesitated, licking his lips nervously. "I like hearing about Jesus, but I can't follow Him right now. My relatives would be angry with me. Later on, if many others enter the Jesus way, I'll join them."

Peng was very disappointed. Walking home with Lam that afternoon he tried to reassure him that Jesus could keep his family safe from the evil spirits, but Lam was filled with doubt and fear.

"My wife doesn't want to believe in Jesus," he said. "She might even leave me if I became a Christian. My parents would also be angry with me, and life would be very difficult."

Peng decided it was good that he himself was still unmarried, free to do whatever he wished with his life. He realized he was fortunate that his father was so tolerant of his new faith. Lately Samat had even asked him questions about the true God, and one afternoon he had listened eagerly to several verses from the Bible.

"God's words seem true," his father had admitted that day. "Perhaps this would be a good way for all Taway to follow, but we must be sure it is safe. I'll watch a while longer to see if Jesus can really protect you from the power of the spirits."

The next time Peng visited the missionaries they gave him a small portable phonograph and some Gospel records. When the Taway people heard music coming from Peng's field house they crowded inside with excitement. They saw only a little black box, but it was singing! They were fascinated by the plate-like object that circled round and round on top as the sound came out. Each time a record finished they begged Peng to rewind the phonograph and play it again.

Peng was delighted at this response, but he did wish the preaching and singing were in the Taway language instead of Laotian, so his friends could understand what they were hearing.

After a few days the adults lost interest, but many young people and children continued to come and listen. Peng wasn't allowed to take the phonograph into the main village but every afternoon, after their work in the fields, a crowd would gather in the field house to hear the records. And the longer they listened the more they understood.

The children especially liked the story of the lost sheep. None of them had ever seen a sheep, but the bleating sound coming from the mysterious box made it clear an animal was in distress. They learnt to count the sheep along with the shepherd and then hold their breath in suspense as he searched everywhere for the missing one. At first they didn't know many of the Lao words, but Peng translated the story into the Taway language, telling it over and over until they understood. Then he would explain that they themselves were lost in sin and Jesus was the Good Shepherd searching for them.

Peng's thirteen-year-old cousin Dee came to listen nearly every day. His parents had died when he was small, and now he lived with an aunt and uncle. He often felt lonely and unwanted, but when Peng said that Jesus loved him and wanted to protect him from harm, Dee's heart would grow warm and his eyes would shine with joy. Sometimes another distant relative named Sahn would also come to listen, and soon he decided to join Peng in following Jesus. How delighted Peng was about that!

The Laotian hymn on one record soon became a favorite. Although the children understood only a few of the words, they soon had them memorized, because the Laotian melody was so easy to sing. "The Lord has come, oh sing with praise, with a heart full of joy, for the Savior came." The music echoed across the rice fields nearly every afternoon and evening, cheering Peng's heart and giving him hope that soon many of his people would begin to walk the Jesus road.

★   ★   ★   ★

The rains stopped in October, and by November the rice was ready to be harvested. Everyone moved back to their field houses, and children worked beside their parents from dawn until late afternoon each day. Grandparents who were too feeble to work in the fields cared for the smaller children and cooked the meals.

Peng was cutting the rice stalks and laying them out to dry in the sun. He worked steadily without pausing, although sweat was rolling down his bare back. His thin cloth cap fitted snugly over his short hair and kept the perspiration from dripping into his eyes. Suk and Ying were in a field nearby, tying dried stalks in bundles to be carried to the threshing floor near their field house.

Peng glanced over at his father working in the distance. If only Samat would acknowledge that Jesus had given them a good crop this year! Silently, as he continued working, Peng thanked God for His blessing and prayed that soon his father would believe in the Savior. Sahn had trusted in Jesus; surely Samat would be the next one to believe?

Now that the harvest had begun there was very little time to study God's words. The family was all back in the field house, and at the end of a long day's work everyone was exhausted and went to bed soon after eating supper. Peng tried to study his Bible in the evenings, but sometimes his eyes wouldn't stay open. It was too dark to read when he first got up in the mornings, because they began work in the fields before daylight. In the small crowded hut there was no privacy to pray aloud, and he found it difficult to concentrate when he prayed silently for very long, although all through the day his thoughts would burst out in short conversations with God.

Often in the evenings he could hear the young men singing over in the field where the girls had their temporary little huts. But this year he had no desire to join them. Since his unhappy experience with Lansee Peng had lost his interest in girls, though the bitterness in his heart had faded. He realized that many things that went on among the youth were immoral and contrary to the teachings of Jesus, and he had decided to wait a few years before considering marriage.

Pausing in his work, Peng straightened his back and stretched. Harvesting was tiring work! He noticed the sun was high above him and it was time for their morning meal.

As they were eating the snails, rice, and peppers Suk had prepared, they heard a voice call across the fields, "Come to a meeting at headman Tuat's house! Enemy soldiers are marching toward the town of Mong!"

Peng and Samat finished eating quickly and hurried to join the men who were gathering near Tuat's field house. Everyone was talking excitedly, discussing the rumors they had heard. Soon the headman came outside and squatted on the porch above them. The crowd grew silent as Tuat held up his hand.

"There is no real danger to us, but we must be alert as we work this afternoon," he said. "The colonel in town sent a messenger to tell us that the rebel army is advancing toward Mong and this area from the north. The Royal Laotian army has gone out to stop them. We are to report immediately if we see any strangers in our area."

Everyone began talking at once when the headman paused. He put up his hand and waited until the people grew silent again.

"I'll appoint some men to hide in the forest surrounding our village and fields tonight to guard us from the enemy and warn us if anyone approaches. This afternoon we'll work as usual. There's no real danger yet, but we must all be watchful."

12

Life Through Death

As the hot afternoon hours slowly passed, Peng kept thinking about the missionaries in town. Surely the women would be frightened? They might even leave!

After he stopped work that afternoon he went to see Tuat. The headman was sitting on his porch. He frowned when he saw Peng waiting to speak to him, and his eyes looked fierce under his thick brows.

"Come on up the ladder," he said. "What do you want?" Tuat was friendly and well liked by the entire village, but Peng felt a bit nervous.

"Would you like me to go into Mong tomorrow?" he asked. "I could find out the latest news and report to you tomorrow evening."

"You're not afraid to go alone?" the headman asked gruffly.

Peng shook his head. Tuat looked thoughtful, then smiled. "Good! The other men are needed here, but if you wish, you may go. You can take a message to the colonel for me."

Samat was upset when Peng reported his plans. "It's dangerous, and we need you here," he said. He didn't mention the missionaries, although he realized that probably Peng's main concern was to see them. With a sigh of exasperation he decided not to forbid him to go, but secretly he was proud that he had volunteered for the errand. At least his son wasn't a coward.

When Peng reached the missionaries' home the next morning he saw a white man preaching to a group of tribal people in the reception room. Where were the foreign women, he wondered. Had they left? He felt very anxious but could not interrupt the meeting. Squatting down behind the crowd to listen, he noticed that several men in the audience were of the Huay tribe. They wore loincloths made of black material with red stripes. Some Huay women sat nearby wearing skirts and blouses of a similar material, with strings of colored beads around their necks and wrists.

The people over on the left side of the room were obviously from the Denah tribe. They were dressed more poorly, except for the large wooden ornaments in their ear lobes. One woman wore ivory plugs nearly two inches in diameter. Peng also saw an elderly man whose legs were tattooed from the mid-thighs to the ankles. The custom of tattooing was dying out in all the tribes, although some still believed it gave protection from injury by bullets. Others thought tattooing was beautiful and would help in obtaining a wife, but Peng had never liked it.

When the foreigner had finished preaching and the crowd had dispersed, Peng introduced himself.

"Oh, I've been wanting to meet you! I'm David

Henriksen," the man said. "I've come here to make Gospel records in the tribal languages around Mong."

Hearing Peng's familiar voice, Anna came in from the kitchen. "It's good to see you, Peng," she said. "When Kathy and Rosemary get back from visiting in Ban Tay, we'll eat lunch together." She explained that Kathy was a new missionary who had recently come to live with them.

"Did you hear about the fighting east of town?" Peng asked anxiously.

Anna nodded and admitted they had been a bit frightened. "We packed our rucksacks and then spent part of the night praying, and God gave us peace so that we finally went to bed and slept. We never did hear any gunshots."

David said, "I've heard that the government soldiers will be coming back to Mong tonight. The rebel troops retreated east toward Vietnam before there was much fighting. Perhaps they were just testing the resistance in our area."

Most of the missionaries had become used to wild rumors and a crisis now and then, for the calm, stoical attitude of the Laotians helped to reassure them. Usually they found the slow country life in Laos rather peaceful in spite of the gathering storm clouds of war.

David told Peng he was sleeping in the army camp on the other side of town. "It wouldn't look right for me to stay here with the women at night," he explained. "I'd like to be here to protect them if the rebels should attack the town, but we have to be careful to avoid all appearance of evil. Otherwise people might think we Christians have the same low standards they do."

"Don't worry about it. God will take care of us," Anna said, and the other women nodded. Peng could see they weren't afraid. He smiled at David.

"Can you visit my village while you're here?" he asked. "I want my family to hear about Jesus, and I can't explain God's words to them very well myself."

"I'll be glad to visit if I can get a travel pass," David answered, "but the local police won't let me go out into the countryside much right now because of the fighting and possible danger. I've had to find men here in town to help me record the Gospel messages in the tribal languages."

"But how do the men know what to say?" Peng looked puzzled. "The tribes in this area don't know anything about Jesus."

"I tell them what to say in Laotian, then they translate it into their own language." As David explained the procedure Peng's face lit up.

"Will you make some recordings in my language, too?" he asked.

"I made two Taway recordings last week," David said. "I had no way to contact you, so I found some men here in town to help me. Do you know Len and Kum?"

"Yes, they live south of my village. But they don't believe in Jesus."

"I wish you could have been here to help me, but the men did speak Taway quite clearly," the missionary said. "I have a way to check that they translated the messages correctly. If you can stay awhile you could watch me do some recording in another language this afternoon, and see how it's done."

"Yes, I'd like to do that," Peng said.

They ate dinner together, and as the dishes were being cleared away a Denah named Cham arrived. David arranged his tape recorder and papers on the table and sat down opposite the tribal man. Peng watched from across the room as the missionary said a sentence in Laotian and asked Cham to translate it into his own language. The tape recorder was running as the man mumbled a few words. After rewinding the tape David played it back, and Cham stared at the black box, wondering how his voice had been trapped inside.

"Now tell me in Laotian what you just said in Denah," David requested. The translation back into Laotian didn't satisfy him so he repeated the entire procedure. After several attempts Cham began to speak more clearly and confidently. Finally David was satisfied, and they went on to the next sentence.

It took a long time to record a short message about how to walk the Jesus road. Peng listened carefully. He understood some of the Denah language and could tell Cham was doing a good job. After an hour he slipped away quietly and returned home, wondering how soon the Taway tape recordings would be made into records that he could play for his friends.

After several visits to the police station David was able to obtain a travel pass to Ban Dao. Following the directions Peng had given him, he arrived in the village one morning and was taken to Samat's field house.

When the neighbors saw the white man talking to Peng on the porch, they stopped their work and came to visit. David chatted with them about the harvest, and they were impressed with his friendliness. After Suk had served him a pumpkin *keng* and rice for lunch, David preached for nearly an hour about the true God and His Son Jesus. Samat said little but he listened carefully, observing that the foreigner seemed humble and kind and his teachings were interesting.

Late that afternoon Peng escorted the missionary back to the motor road, eager to have some time alone with him to get better acquainted. He was surprised when he learned that David was unmarried. The missionary admitted he was sometimes lonely, but he felt it was more important right then to travel about the country making recordings so that more tribes could hear the Gospel in their own language. He explained it would be difficult to do this work if he had a wife and children to care for.

"I'm like a grain of wheat or rice," he said. "The grain must be buried in the ground and die in order for there to be a harvest." He paused at the side of the trail and opened his Bible to show Peng where Jesus had said such words.[1]

Then David concluded, "I can multiply myself if I give up my will like Jesus did, and spend my life to win others. When it's God's time for me to find a wife, He will provide the right one for me."

Peng thought about this later as he was harvesting the rice. He cut a stalk and looked at it carefully, realizing that the many grains hanging from the head of the stalk came from one single grain of rice which had been buried in the ground. An earnest look of determination came into his eyes, and he resolved right then that he would serve God faithfully even if it meant staying unmarried, so that someday there might be many, many Taway following Jesus. And if he ever married, it would have to be to a Christian girl who would gladly join him in spreading God's Word in his tribe.

A few weeks later when Peng went to Mong he was amazed to discover the town was crowded with a new regiment of soldiers! There had been another attack by rebel soldiers who had got quite close this time. The missionaries told him they had heard heavy shelling and had been warned to be ready to evacuate quickly if it became necessary. But mortar fire had apparently scared off the enemy, who had disappeared when government troops began to advance

[1] John 12:24-26

towards them. The missionaries were full of praise to God for His deliverance.

"I wondered if I would ever see you again," Rosemary told Peng. "But it has worked out for good, because there are several Christians among the soldiers who've come to defend the town. They are lonely for Christian fellowship and are coming to church regularly to study the Bible with us."

Peng was delighted to see the room filled with soldiers when church began. He particularly enjoyed meeting Kham, a Christian policeman who had been to Bible School. He knew how to preach and could explain difficult Bible verses and answer many of Peng's questions.

But Satan never concedes defeat easily, and he now began to use extreme physical weariness and other distractions to hinder the effectiveness of the missionaries. The women felt weighed down by a vague sense of spiritual darkness and frustration, as they continued to give out the Word of God.

One Sunday a Swiss representative of the Red Cross arrived in the middle of the church service, wanting to ask the missionaries for help in distributing food and clothing to tribal refugees who had come out of the war-torn area near the South Vietnamese border. He was startled to see a group of Laotian soldiers studying the Bible at the dining room table, their machine guns stacked under the table by their feet.

Unwilling to interrupt the Bible study, Anna

handed him a French Bible to read until the church service was over. After the soldiers left she listened to his request and agreed to help him, then began explaining the Gospel in French, although he assured her he was religious and trying his best to do good works. It took him a while to comprehend that being a Christian in the true Bible sense was something quite different.

Although the Christian soldiers rarely discussed the progress of the war with the missionaries, they did tell them some hair-raising stories. Some of their friends in the army had sold themselves to Satan in order to gain protection from harm, and when the enemy's bullets missed them, these men gave the credit to the devil. Many soldiers carried little idols of Buddha with them all the time, believing that no bullet could kill them if they were wearing such a charm.

One day when Peng was visiting, a Christian soldier named Laht came to use the missionaries' iron. They took some red-hot charcoal from the kitchen stove and filled the old-fashioned iron for him. When it was hot enough he pressed his uniform and then left hurriedly.

Peng looked puzzled. "Doesn't Laht pray?" he asked. "Why didn't he pray before he left?" He had taken seriously the teaching he had heard on a Gospel record encouraging him to pray after awakening in the morning and before going to bed, before eating or working, before going on a journey, and always when meeting with other Christians. He had thought all believers would do this.

By mid-December the military situation around Mong had greatly improved, and the local colonel gave the missionaries permission to go out to some of the villages in the country.

"Would you like us to come to your village?" Rosemary asked Peng one Sunday. "The colonel says it's safe now."

"Oh, yes, come as soon as you can!" Peng answered, his face beaming with joy. But he warned them they shouldn't plan to stay overnight. "It might be dangerous for you to be out in the countryside after dark. Anyway, you would have to spend the night in our field house, which is small and has only one room. The village headman won't allow foreigners to sleep in the main village. Our people think it would offend the spirits," he explained.

"That's all right," Anna said. "If your parents are there too, it wouldn't look bad for us to be sleeping in the same room."

"We don't have beds. We sleep on mats on the floor."

"We don't mind," Rosemary assured him. "We've spent the night in many village homes, and we're used to how people live in the country. But we won't stay overnight this time. The colonel wants us to return to town before dark."

So one December morning Peng welcomed them joyfully to the field house and took them inside to meet his parents. Suk had made a large *keng* with some shrimps and tiny fish that Ying had caught in a pond near the river. A leafy green vegetable had been cooked with the fish, and the missionaries found this very tasty over their rice.

"The Taway people eat differently from the Lao, do they?" Anna asked, seeing the brightly colored enamel plates and pewter spoons for everyone.

"Yes, we do," said Peng. "The Lao and many of the other hill tribes eat steamed glutinous rice, rolling it into a ball with their fingers and then dipping it in the stew. But we boil our rice and like to use spoons."

A crowd gathered on the porch of the small house to watch the missionaries eat. Many of the people had never seen a white woman before. Children giggled softly at the women's pale faces and large noses, for they had seen only brown faces and small round noses in their village. But everyone listened respectfully when the missionaries began talking about the true God.

Only a few of those present understood Laotian, but Peng translated everything into the Taway language for them. Sahn had brought his older brother; he hadn't come to church in town for a long time, but he said he was still following the Jesus way. Samat and Suk listened quietly, marveling at Peng as he lovingly and firmly explained the missionaries' words. Obviously the foreign women respected him. Samat didn't understand why, but he felt proud of his son that day. The message of Jesus sounded good, although he still doubted it could be true. He listened thoughtfully and was friendly toward the three missionary women, inviting them to come again soon.

★　　★　　★　　★

Peng looked discouraged when he visited Mong two weeks later.

"Sahn has gone back to the old ways," he reported. "Our village had a big feast last week, and his father insisted he make an offering to appease the spirits. He gave in, so now I'm the only Christian in the village again."

"But God won't cast him away if he has truly believed in Jesus," Rosemary said. "When God gives us eternal life, it doesn't last only until we do something bad. Jesus will bring Sahn back to Himself if he has truly been born into God's family."

Peng's eyes lit up with new hope. "Of course! Just like God forgave me when I failed Him. How can I help Sahn turn back to the right path?"

Rosemary opened her Bible and read several verses that might help him. Peng especially liked the words in Hebrews 13:5-6, "For He has said, I will never leave you, nor forsake you. So we may boldly say, The Lord is my helper, and I will not fear what man can do to me."

"How would you say that in your language?" Rosemary asked. As Peng translated the verses, the missionaries attempted to write the Taway words in Laotian script. It was difficult to decide how to spell some of the strange sounds, but they finally had a rough translation that they could read back to Peng with fair accuracy.

"I wish we could stay here permanently and learn your language," Rosemary told Peng, and he nodded eagerly. "God will work it out if that's His will."

After they had studied together for several hours, Anna said, "We've promised to visit a tribal village north of here tomorrow. A man named Sung has invited us. The last time we went there the people were having a feast and he was drunk, but he has promised that this time he will have the headman and all the villagers assembled for a meeting. Would you go with us and help preach? You could probably sleep at our Vietnamese neighbor's house tonight."

"I'd like that," Peng said. "I'll go with you anytime you need me. I get very lonesome in my village without any Christian friends."

They left at dawn the next morning after a quick breakfast together. It wasn't a long walk, but the trail was difficult to find at times, and the missionaries were grateful for Peng's company. They were pleased too that he could understand the tribal language, although it was different from his own. He helped preach at the village, exhorting Sung and the others to follow God with all their hearts, speaking with confidence and conviction but also with a gentle, loving manner.

As they walked home Rosemary told Peng it was nearly Christmas, the time when Christians all over the world celebrated Jesus' birth. She invited him to join them on Christmas Day for a worship service and a simple meal.

Peng was excited and eager to see what the Christians did on their festival days.

"Of course I'll come!" he declared. "Maybe Sahn will come with me if he decides to turn back to the Jesus way."

13

Fellowship

ON CHRISTMAS DAY, Peng and Sahn got a late start, arriving in town past noontime. Since the missionaries had expected them earlier, the food was already cooked and ready to serve. But Kham, the Christian policeman, arrived just then, eager to help Sahn come back to God. He counseled him for nearly an hour until at last Sahn prayed to God for forgiveness for making a sacrifice to the evil spirits.

Finally at about two o'clock that afternoon they sat down to eat Christmas dinner together. By then the roast chicken was cold, but it was still delicious served with rice and hot peppers, Peng thought. Rosemary had made a "pumpkin" pie with some canned sweet potatoes. The men tasted this strange food cautiously and decided they liked it, although they weren't used to eating many sweet foods. They ate heartily, using their forks awkwardly as they followed the women's example. Afterward Peng insisted on helping to clear the table, and then they spent the next few hours reading God's Word, singing Laotian hymns of praise, and just enjoying one another's company. When Kham had to return to work, the tribal men lingered on.

"Do you have many large towns in your

country?" Sahn asked Rosemary. "How is your country different from ours?" It was hard for him and Peng to comprehend electric lights, automatic washing machines, and telephones, for they had never seen these things even in the town of Mong.

Peng asked Anna, "Are you going to get married someday? Why haven't you found a husband yet?"

Anna blushed and bowed her head. She didn't answer for a minute, and Peng thought he might have offended her. Her straight dark hair pulled back into a tight bun made her almost look like a Laotian, and she spoke the language so well that at times he forgot she was a foreigner.

"I'm sorry," he said at last. "I shouldn't ask such questions."

"It's all right," Anna said slowly. "I just don't know how to explain it to you. Actually I was engaged until last year, but then I realized that person wasn't God's choice for me, so now we're not going to get married after all."

Peng thought about that for a few minutes. "How did you know he wasn't God's choice for you?" he asked.

"I didn't have peace in my heart about marrying him. He was a Christian and was even serving God, but I suddenly realized I didn't really love him and that God wanted me to stay single."

Sahn, who had been listening carefully, looked puzzled. "But everyone should get married!" he exclaimed. "Isn't Kathy getting married this week?" The women had told him Kathy had gone to visit her fiancé Ron in Savannakhet.

"No, they won't get married for several months yet," Rosemary said. "First they both want to learn to speak the Laotian language really well, and they can spend more time studying if they are single."

Peng was astounded that the women would sacrifice their personal desires just to bring the good news of Jesus to Laos. It would have been so much easier for them to stay in their homeland, near their family and friends.

"Is everyone already a Christian in your country?" he asked.

"No. Most people in America have heard of Jesus but many of them aren't willing to follow Him," Rosemary explained. "And there are still some groups in my country who haven't heard about Jesus yet. I used to work among the Navajo Indians. They live out in the desert, far from the cities, and many of the older Indians still follow their tribal religion. Many of them have never even learned to speak or understand the English language."

Sahn's eyes widened in surprise. "Why did you leave them and come to Laos?" he asked.

"Because there are many missionaries already living among them, and I realized that some countries like Laos didn't have enough workers to spread the Gospel adequately."

"How did you hear about our country?" Peng inquired.

Rosemary smiled. "I read about it in a magazine while I was on the ship coming to our mission headquarters in Singapore. Then I began to pray that God would send me here to Laos, and eventually the mission leaders agreed."

"Do you mean you left home without knowing where you were going to serve God?" Peng stared at Rosemary in astonishment.

"Yes, in a way. I knew I was going to stay in Singapore for a while to get my assignment, but I wasn't sure at first where God would send me after that. But I had peace in my heart because I knew I was obeying God and that He would choose the right place for me. And He did! I'm so glad He brought me here to your country."

"I'm glad I'm here, too," Anna agreed, and both women smiled warmly at Peng and Sahn. Peng saw real love in their eyes. His heart sang with joy. These were his true sisters, for even though their homelands and customs were quite different from his, Jesus had brought them together and made them into one family.

As he walked home with Sahn late that afternoon Peng kept thinking about what the women had told them. He decided that he would not get married until he found a tribal girl who loved Jesus like these women did and was willing to give up everything to serve God. Surely someday soon many Taway people would trust in Jesus, and God would provide a Christian wife for him. In the meantime he would try to follow Jesus and obey Him with all his heart as the missionaries did.

A few days after Christmas Peng's brother came home for a brief visit. Everyone looked at him in awe. It was obvious he had been living with foreigners, for he dressed differently and even talked differently. Samat was upset when he heard that Khap had been digging holes for the Lao Publique. He was amazed, and also relieved, that the evil spirits had not punished him for this. Khap seemed prosperous and in good health.

Khap was impressed by the change in his older brother, for although Peng was feeling ill that week, he radiated peace and confidence and refused to make an offering to the spirits. Even his bitterness toward Lansee and his short temper had disappeared. Khap thought Peng seemed like a new person.

Curious about the foreign women who had been teaching his brother, Khap stopped by to see them one day when he was in town. He listened politely as they explained the Gospel message, but his ambitions to obtain wealth and success left no room for religion. The following week he returned to his job in the city.

Soon after Christmas things began to change in Mong, as many of the Christian soldiers were transferred elsewhere. Only Kham continued to join Peng each Sunday for fellowship and teaching at the mission station. Kham was now stationed across the river, living on the grounds of a Buddhist temple. He found many opportunities to witness to the monks there and was grateful for a quiet atmosphere in which to study his Bible, so different from the army camp. One Sunday he confided to the missionaries that he had joined the police because he didn't want to engage in warfare, but now all policemen had been made part of the Laotian army. Although he didn't like fighting, he said he would carry out his responsibilities faithfully and try to be an example for Christ wherever he was.

Another day Kham arrived with a big smile on his face. "The soldiers have been complaining because they haven't received any wages for three months," he reported. "I've been telling them not to worry, because I knew Jesus would send the money this month in answer to my prayers. The money came this week, and now my friends know that Jesus has great power."

In mid-January Peng became quite ill, and his mother and sister went to ask the missionaries for some medicine. Suk was fascinated by the foreigner's cupboard of dishes and their way of cooking. She and Ying taught the missionaries several Taway words as they chatted and laughed together in the kitchen, watching Rosemary knead bread dough and set it out to rise.

A few days later Anna and Rosemary walked out to Ban Dao with more medicine for Peng and also some new records. These Gospel records, made many months ago, had just arrived from America, one in Taway and another in a different closely related tribal language which the people would be able to understand. The tapes David had made in November had been sent to California to be made into records, but these had not yet been shipped to Laos.

Following the short-cut Peng had showed them, it was only twelve kilometers to the house in the paddy fields. Soon after the women arrived a crowd gathered to stare at them and listen to the new records. Sahn was among them, smiling happily, eager for fellowship.

Anna gave Peng and several others an injection for yaws. Although Samat was also ill, he wouldn't take any medicine. Rosemary told the story of Lazarus and the rich man, explaining that after he died the rich man still loved his relatives and even begged that someone go tell them to repent: The Taway audience was impressed, agreeing that it was logical that their ancestors should not want to harm them after death. But when urged to follow Jesus, they shook their heads in fear.

"I want to follow Jesus," said a small voice. It was Dee, Peng's orphaned cousin. He was a thin, frail-looking boy who looked much younger than his fourteen years. Rosemary talked with him, and then he prayed inviting Jesus into his heart.

"Do you believe Jesus has entered your heart and saved you?" she asked him afterward.

"Yes!" Dee answered with conviction, a bright smile lighting his thin face. Samat had been listening carefully to the conversation but he said nothing.

After eating the delicious *keng* and rice Suk

had cooked, the women rested awhile, getting better acquainted with Samat and Suk. When they left, Peng walked across the fields with them.

"At last one of my close relatives has trusted in Jesus!" he exclaimed. "Maybe my father will be the next one to believe."

A few days later Peng brought his father to the mission station, explaining that Samat had finally gone to the Filipino clinic for treatment of his cough and chest pain.

"The doctor wants him to stay here in town so he can go back for medicine tomorrow and the next day," Peng told the women. "He can sleep at a house near the clinic, but they can't feed him. Could he eat with you while he's in town?"

"Of course he can! We'll be glad to have you," Rosemary said to Samat, pleased to be able to minister to him. For the next three days she served him tasty Laotian *kengs* with rice twice a day when he came over from the clinic.

As the women chatted with Samat each day and told him more about Jesus, they noticed he was showing an increasing interest in the Gospel, and they felt sure he would soon become a Christian. However, he had made no decision when Peng and Dee came to take him home at the end of the week.

Early in February, a few days after Kathy returned from Savannakhet, the women visited Ban Dao again. This time they stayed overnight, as the countryside was peaceful again and considered quite safe by the local authorities. Their neighbor took them halfway in his truck, so they had to walk only six kilometers and arrived at the field house soon after eight o'clock in the morning.

They were eager to see the mountain village, so Peng took them up the rocky hillside to meet his married sister Noy. He also introduced them to the family his cousin Dee was living with, but no one in the village wanted to hear about Jesus.

The missionaries were impressed with the natural beauty of Ban Dao. It was like a huge rock garden in the shadow of the steep mountain, on the first hilly rise above the plains. There was scarcely a flat place in the entire village, even the path being made of stepping stones as it wound among the tall stilt-legged houses shaded by clusters of banana trees and every kind of palm tree. However, it was not a happy place. The people's faces seemed clouded with fear and suspicion. The missionary women felt oppressed by gloom and sadness as they saw near every house a fetish of chicken feathers and bamboo, proclaiming allegiance to the spirits of darkness.

As they walked back to the field house Peng reported sadly that Sahn had again turned back to demon worship because of pressure from his relatives.

"I'm sorry to hear that," Rosemary told him. "If God hadn't prepared your heart to seek the truth, there probably wouldn't be one

Christian among your people today. Satan seems to have great power here."

Peng's parents had not quite finished harvesting their rice, so they were still living in the field house. They welcomed the women eagerly and were pleased that they could stay overnight. That evening a group of young people crowded inside the small bamboo hut to listen to the missionaries and play the Gospel records. The one record in the Taway language was already well worn, but everyone seemed to enjoy the Laotian records as well. In fact, they had memorized three hymns from one record even though they didn't understand all of the Lao words. Christian words had been set to Lao folk tunes, and the young people found the melodies captivating.

For several hours they enthusiastically sang the hymns over and over, just as they had been doing every night for weeks. It grew late, and finally Peng tried to persuade them to stop so the missionaries could sleep, but the teenagers weren't tired yet. They sang one final hymn again, all four verses from memory.

At last the young people said goodbye and began to climb down the ladder from the porch, regrouping in the darkness outside. Some of them continued singing there for nearly an hour, reluctant to go home. Their tribal religion had never provided such happy songs and delightful entertainment as this! Lying on their mats in the small bamboo house, the weary missionaries longed to get some sleep as it was near midnight, but their hearts were filled with praise to God as they listened to the Gospel message echoing across the paddy fields. Though there were still only three Christians here, God was obviously working in the Taway tribe.

The next morning Peng led the women to Khang village, where the Taway record had been made the previous year. The village was deserted, but eventually they located the people working out in their fields. No one wanted to listen, except a few small children who had gathered to play in an old deserted schoolhouse on the hillside.

Afterwards they went to Peng's family's garden and met his crippled Uncle Vahn. Peng explained that during the feast days when the spirits were being appeased it was taboo for a crippled person to enter the mountain village. Rather than be forced to leave periodically, Vahn spent most of his time down by the garden where he had everything he needed. He lived alone in an old granary, did blacksmith work, and tended the garden for his brother Samat. He was delighted to have visitors, and the women talked with him a long time before they left to return home.

When Peng came to town for church the next Sunday, Rosemary told him she had received a letter asking her to help with the Youth Camp and Bible School, and soon after that she would be leaving for a year's furlough in America.

"Kathy, Anna, and I will be counselors at the Youth Camp," she told Peng. "We'll have to leave here soon and we won't be able to return, but someone else will come to take our place in March or April. We're not sure yet whom the mission leaders will send, but we hope it will be a married couple so you will have a man to teach you."

Peng looked downcast. He didn't want his friends to leave. His parents weren't Christians yet! "What is Youth Camp?" he asked.

Rosemary started to explain, then she stopped and looked at Kathy, her eyes sparkling. Kathy began to smile. She had the same idea. "Maybe Peng could go to Youth Camp!" she exclaimed. "Surely he'll be able to get a travel pass, for there's not much fighting in the countryside right now."

Peng was excited, for Youth Camp sounded like fun. He suddenly realized there must be many other Christians in Laos. Now he would meet some of them and learn more about the wonderful God who had changed his life! Then maybe when he came home he would be able to persuade his father to join him in following Jesus.

14

Youth Camp

THE WHIRRING OF the helicopter blades grew louder. Peng's seat gave a lurch and suddenly the treetops outside disappeared, and he could see only blue sky. A soldier sat in front of him at the open door of the helicopter with a machine gun pointed toward the ground, his eyes scanning the jungle for signs of the enemy.

As the noisy machine banked for a turn, Mong lay stretched out below them, the river curving around the town like a silver ribbon. Peng gripped the edge of his seat and felt thankful for the belt which held him down firmly in place. Without it he was sure he would slide out of the doorway onto the ground below.

Most of the other passengers seemed calm, so he tried to relax. On his right three soldiers guarded a man wearing a Denah loincloth. The prisoner's hands were tied behind him, his eyes glazed with fear. Peng supposed he had been caught spying or helping the rebel army.

As they neared the mountains Peng thought he could see Taway villages far below him, the round clearings strung like a necklace of brown nuts through the emerald green forest. Stretching his head forward to get a good look, he wondered which one was his own village. The houses in the clearings were small and hard to recognize from where he was, so high above the ground. How tiny they must appear to the Creator, who could see the whole earth at one moment!

Peng's heart flooded with gratitude that God had reached out and found him. A year ago he had been living in superstitious fear of evil spirits, but now he was free from such bondage and was on his way to Youth Camp where he would meet many others who loved Jesus!

At first it had seemed impossible for him to go, for travel permits and transportation were difficult to obtain. But the missionaries had helped him obtain a pass from the local police, and a friendly Laotian army officer had made it possible for him to have this free ride to Solane. Bus travel between Mong and Solane had stopped now because of the war.

Midway over the mountain the helicopter began to descend. It landed in a large field, and a group of soldiers waiting nearby ran over to talk with the pilot. Peng couldn't hear what they said, as the helicopter blades were still spinning noisily. After a moment four soldiers began to climb inside. The man with the machine gun motioned to Peng to get out, and the soldier sitting next to him gave him a shove.

"You'll have to get out here at Kong. We don't have room to take you any further," he said.

Gripping his small bundle Peng jumped down to the ground and stood there, bewildered. Suddenly the helicopter was gone, rising high above him.

He looked around, wondering where he should go. He decided the village must be some distance away, for there were only a few houses in sight. Silently asking God to guide him, he walked over to a large two-story building at the edge of the field, but found it was closed up and empty. He recalled suddenly that two of the missionary women he had known in Mong had been transferred here. But where were they?

He was still standing uncertainly in front of the house when a man came hurrying up the path.

"*Sambai baw*! Are you looking for the missionaries?" he asked.

"*Sambai dee*! Yes, where are they?" Peng explained who he was and that he was on the way to the Youth Camp.

"The women teachers had to go to Solane for a few weeks," the man told him. "I'm Lum, the pastor of the church here. Are you a Christian?"

Soon they were good friends. Peng learned there was a Huay village nearby, and a small group of believers.

"Come stay at my house," Lum insisted. "You can ride down to Solane on Tuesday in the mail jeep. The missionaries there will help you get to Youth Camp."

The next day was Sunday. Ten adults and a few children came to the church service which was held in the pastor's house. Lum led the singing, read some Scripture, and then discussed the verses briefly. At the conclusion he announced that Peng had asked to be baptized, since there was no one to do this for him in Mong.

"First tell everyone how you became a Christian," Lum requested.

Peng moved to the front of the crowded room and sat on the mat beside the pastor. He told how he had searched for the truth, certain that a great and good spirit had made the world. Concluding with the story of his visit to John and Dorothy when he had asked Jesus into his heart, he added, "God has been good to me. I'm so glad He brought me here to Kong so I can be baptized today. For a time my cousin Dee was the only Taway Christian beside me, although my friend Sahn did follow Jesus for a while. Now there is one more: Nuen, one of my relatives who lives in the potter's village, believed in Jesus a few days ago. My uncle Vahn lives near there and he too is close to believing. But my father is a spirit priest and still fears the forest spirits. Please pray for him."

After praying for God's blessing on Peng and his relatives, the Huay believers went down to the river at the edge of the village, just a short walk away, and watched as the pastor baptized him. Returning to Lum's house afterward, all the Christians joined in remembering the Savior's death as they observed the Lord's supper. Peng listened carefully as Lum explained that the crackers and red juice he passed around represented Jesus' body and shed blood. It was wonderful to be part of the family of God!

Late Monday afternoon a jeep arrived with mail and a few supplies for the local shopkeeper. When the driver returned to Solane the next morning, Peng went with him. The rutted road followed the narrow ridge of the mountain, tunneling through high grass that swayed in the wind above their heads. The ruts that had been made in the rainy season were so deep that most of the time the driver kept to the edge of the narrow road, tipping the jeep alarmingly to one side.

Finally the tortuous road began to descend the western side of the mountains, winding down a steep grade past villages and coffee plantations. Peng began to feel ill as the jeep sped around the sharp curves, but at last the road leveled out and they drove into Solane. It was a much larger town than he had ever seen.

His legs felt stiff when he climbed down and said goodbye to the driver. He had never ridden in a vehicle for five hours before. Flinching from the crowd of noisy people surging about him, he stared at the row of large buses parked across the street. He hoped the missionary women had arrived from Mong by now. Otherwise he wouldn't know one person in this town except his brother Khap – if he was still here!

Bravely he followed the directions he had been given, and after several inquiries along the way he found the mission house, where he was welcomed enthusiastically. Although his missionary friends had not yet arrived, the foreign teachers here seemed to know all about him. "We've been praying for you nearly a year now," they said as they gathered round him joyously. "Tell us about your trip and how God is working in your village."

That night Peng slept in the home of a Christian Lao family, and during the next few days he made many new friends among the believers in Solane. They helped him locate his brother Khap who had a job driving a truck for some Americans.

Khap was eager to hear the news from home, but he impatiently interrupted when Peng began to speak about Jesus. "I've heard about Jesus," he said. "Some of these foreigners use His name like a swear word. They don't seem to worship Him or fear Him at all, and I'm not interested in Him."

Khap had a busy schedule and didn't have time to visit the missionaries. He showed Peng his wrist watch and new clothes, and generously gave him some money. He even went to the marketplace with him and helped him purchase a shirt and tennis shoes imported from Hong Kong. It was nearly noon and most of the market square was deserted, as the food vendors departed by mid-morning, but several rows of stalls in the center of the block were still thronged with shoppers looking for clothes and household items. Peng had never seen such a large market square.

He was amazed at the large number of prosperous Chinese and Vietnamese merchants in Solane. Some of their shops along the street even had glass windows in front instead of folding doors. While waiting several days for his missionary friends to arrive from Mong, he had plenty of time to explore the city.

He puzzled over the odd customs of the people there. Many stayed up until quite late in the evenings, even walking along the streets after dark. There was a narrow strip of concrete along the edges of the main avenues where one could walk to be out of the way of the trucks and cars that roared by at all hours. Some streets were lit up at night with bright lights on tall posts, and even the Lao chapel had strange lights that went on with a flick of a tiny switch. The family he stayed with didn't appear to be especially prosperous, yet they lit a small kerosene lamp in the evenings and let it burn for several hours. This seemed wasteful to Peng at first, but it was pleasant to be able to sit up and chat after dark and read the Bible together.

At last Kathy and Anna arrived. They reported that they had been delayed by illness, and that several people had recently died of typhoid fever in the Mong area. Rosemary had already gone on ahead to prepare Bible lessons for the Youth Camp.

The next day a Swiss missionary named Hermann Christen came by to take Peng up to Savannakhet in his truck. Kathy decided to go with them, but Anna had some important work to do in Solane for a few more days.

"I'll be seeing you at camp next week," Anna promised as Peng climbed into the truck with the missionaries and waved goodbye. During the tedious four-hour trip along the bumpy rutted road, Peng dozed a lot. He was excited, but he wasn't used to riding in a vehicle for so many hours, and it made him sleepy. When he was awake, anxiety gripped him. He was a long way from home and going further every minute! Would he enjoy the Bible camp, and would the Laotian young people be friendly to him?

At last they drove into the town of Savannakhet. Peng shook himself awake and stared at the many concrete, two-story buildings. This town was a lot like Solane, he decided. Finally Hermann turned down a shady street and drove into the front yard of the Mission Evangelique compound.

A tall, slender white man rushed out to greet them. "You must be Peng!" he said. "*Sambai baw*!" Holding his palms together, he ducked his head politely in the proper Laotian way, and then began to chatter eagerly in English with Kathy and Hermann.

As soon as Kathy could interrupt the excited flood of words, she said, "Peng, this is my fiancé Ron. We're going to be married later this year." Peng noticed that Ron's hair and skin were even fairer than Kathy's, but in spite of these oddities he liked *Than* Ron at once.

They spent much of the day together, and Ron introduced him to many of the local Christians, most of whom lived in a village on the edge of town. One friendly family invited Peng to stay with them until Bible camp began. Their oldest son Kee was also going to attend camp, and soon the two boys had hurried down to the river for a bath, and were swimming and playing together like brothers.

On Sunday morning Peng was amazed to see about fifty believers gather for church in the small chapel. A thin, gray-haired farmer led the service and preached about Jesus the Good Shepherd finding the lost sheep. Peng learned he had been the leading elder of this assembly for many years.

Early Tuesday morning Peng walked into town with his new friend Kee, each carrying his bedroll on his shoulder. Already the young people were gathering at the mission compound for the trip to camp. At ten o'clock Ron left with Kathy and Rosemary and a load of Laotian girls in the mission landrover, and a few minutes later Peng and eight Laotian boys climbed into the back of a pickup truck driven by another Swiss missionary, named Armand Heiniger. Along the way they stopped at two small villages and picked up several more boys, until the back of the truck was filled.

Everyone had brought a small bedroll with extra clothes wrapped inside a light blanket. Peng's blanket held only one change of clothing carefully wrapped around his precious Lao Bible and his rubber thongs, but he felt well dressed because he was wearing his new shirt and the canvas shoes Khap had bought him in Solane.

Finally the truck stopped at the edge of a river, where everyone climbed out and looked for the boats that would take them upstream.

Mr. Heiniger announced, "The girls have been taken up to the village in the motorboats and canoes, and it will be several hours before the boats come back. We'll have to walk, but we can leave our bedrolls here, and the boats will take them up to the village with the last load of campers."

During the next two hours Peng wished he had worn his old rubber sandals instead of his new shoes. Most of the trail through the forest was rough and dusty, and they passed several muddy areas where deep shade had kept the path from drying out after the last rain. The shoes rubbed painfully on Peng's feet where they were tender from his recent yaws infection.

But he liked being back in the woods away from the paved roads and the noise of town. He listened with interest as Kee and the other Laotian boys competed in naming various trees and shrubs along the trail, many of which were also common in Peng's province. Several boys entered into a lively discussion of the practical uses of the leaves and berries they saw.

When a sudden rainstorm came up, Peng and his new friends huddled under trees and bushes but were soon drenched, and the path became a quagmire. At last the rain stopped and the sun came out. They hurried on down the narrow path through the trees, singing Christian choruses and hymns. Peng joined in the best he could, his heart warmed by the happy fellowship with others who believed in Jesus.

Finally emerging from the forest, they found themselves on a wide unpaved avenue which led them through the village of Khone. Peng was astonished to see several large wooden houses set back from the road in spacious fenced yards. This seemed to be a prosperous village. He saw Rosemary and Anna in the distance and called out a greeting to them when they waved at him.

"That's the girls' dormitory over there," Kee said. "We'll be staying in one of the homes near the chapel." As soon as they had found their assigned sleeping places, they dashed off for a swim in the river. Peng had fun splashing his new friends with water and swimming out to a log caught in the middle of the stream.

The last group of campers arrived at dusk as they were eating supper. Everyone was tired and went to bed early that night. Peng and the boys from Savannakhet slept in an empty house near the chapel; those from other villages stayed in Christian homes nearby. It was so hot that he didn't need his blanket at all. Someone must have kept a dog in the house once, for he woke up the next morning with flea bites all over him!

The week passed quickly, filled with interesting activities. Peng especially enjoyed the small Bible classes in the mornings and the big group meeting in the chapel after supper. He tried hard to memorize the assigned Bible verses each day. However, some boys talked during class and made no effort to learn. They never opened a Bible in their room at night, and they seemed interested only in having a good time. Peng was puzzled by their attitude until he met a camper named Danee, who explained that many of these boys, like himself, had always known about Jesus Danee's father was pastor of the church there in Khone.

"I've gone to church all my life, and sometimes I get tired of it," he admitted.

Peng was shocked but remained politely silent, remembering how earnestly he had searched for the truth. He hoped he would never take it for granted or forget the many people who had not yet heard of the Savior. He was surprised to learn that almost everyone in the large village of Khone was a believer. Later *Than* Armand told him that the first missionaries to come from Switzerland in 1902 had settled here. In spite of many difficulties they had finally translated the Bible into the Laotian language. One entire family had died of cholera during those early years; Peng saw their gravestones near the river.

Peng was surprised that missionaries had been in Laos so long. He thought, If only they had come to my tribe years ago and preached in my village, then perhaps my parents would already have become Christians!

For supper nearly every evening the campers had bullfrog stew with their rice. Peng heard that most of the Christian families in Khone were rather poor. They worked hard to prepare the meals, but they couldn't afford to butcher a pig or kill enough chickens to feed eighty young people for a week. However, at this time of the year plenty of frogs could be caught down by the river. Although many of the campers complained about the monotony of the meals, Peng thought the *kengs* were delicious. He noticed that the missionaries ate with the young people each evening, and they also seemed to enjoy the food, or at least they didn't complain about eating frog meat in their *keng*.

One evening the campers were pleased to find ant eggs in the *keng* instead of frog meat. This was certainly a welcome change, Peng agreed. He smiled when he saw *Than* Ron give his fellow missionaries a dubious look before tasting the stew hesitantly. Obviously, Americans did not normally eat ant eggs! But *Than* Ron must have liked the taste, because soon he was eating as voraciously as the other campers.

The Laotians served a steamed glutinous rice that was quite different from the boiled rice Peng was used to, and they didn't use spoons, but he soon became adept at eating with his fingers like everyone else. He learned to roll a bit of sticky rice into a ball on the palm of his hand and then dip it into the small bowl of *keng* which he shared with several other boys. The difficult part was quickly to lift out a piece of meat or vegetable with the rice and get it into his mouth before the ball of wet rice disintegrated on his lap. There was much laughter and teasing when some of the newer missionaries had difficulty eating, but most of them had already mastered the technique.

Peng noticed that there were many more girls than boys at the camp. "Most of the boys our age are in the army," Kee explained. "And, of course, a few are in school. But many of us don't want to go to school beyond the sixth grade, and we can't afford it, anyway."

Peng was a few years older than the other campers and only three other boys were tribal like himself, but everyone was friendly to him except some of the girls. A few girls would nod and smile shyly when they passed him on the village paths, but one group of girls treated him as if he was invisible. However, they found excuses to chat with the Laotian boys even though the boys and girls sat on opposite sides of the chapel during meetings and ate all their meals separately. Some of these girls had had their hair cut and curled in the modern Thai fashion, and they were always combing it and primping, obviously more interested in their appearance than in the Bible lessons. Peng knew right away he wouldn't want a girl like that for his wife.

"Do you have a girl friend?" Kee asked him one day.

"No, but I don't think any of these Laotian girls would be interested in me," Peng replied. "And there aren't any Christian girls in my tribe yet, so I guess I won't be getting married very soon."

Kee looked surprised. "But most fellows your age are already married! I'm not so particular. All

I want is a pretty girl who likes me, although it would be nice if she were a believer in Jesus."

"Remember what *Than* Hermann taught us about the dangers of marrying an unbeliever," Peng warned. They had just had a Bible lesson on that subject, but it seemed that Kee hadn't paid much attention. Peng's bitterness toward females had evaporated soon after he had become a Christian, but he still wasn't very interested in marriage. Life seemed complicated enough without getting involved with flighty, changeable girls! And Lao women did not normally marry tribal men, so he would have to wait until there were more Christians in his tribe.

Peng enjoyed not having any responsibilities for once. It was fun just to be a boy again. After watching others play for the first few days he joined in a lively game of dodgeball. He hadn't laughed so much since he was a small boy!

He sometimes watched the missionary men play volleyball, but he didn't attempt to learn that game. Kee and some of the other Lao boys played, but it was too rough for the girls, although Peng saw Rosemary and Anna join in one day. They weren't as expert as the men, but they did hit the ball over the net several times. Finally Anna dropped out of the game, wiping the sweat from her forehead.

"Are you having a good time, Peng?" she asked as she sat down beside him on the grass.

"Oh, yes," he answered. "I'm not very good at some games, but I enjoy the Bible lessons and I've made lots of new friends."

The weather was very hot and after playing ball in the afternoons everyone looked forward to a swim in the river. The girls usually went down to the river first, as they had to help prepare the supper, and the boys liked to play ball a while longer. Several times Peng carried two buckets of water back to camp on a shoulder pole. Some of the boys complained when it was their turn to get the water for drinking and washing, because the women usually did this job at home, but Peng noticed the girls also carried water back to camp when they returned from their time at the river.

Just before supper everyone gathered outside to watch the missionaries act out a Bible story in pantomime, and the campers were asked to guess what story was being illustrated. They laughed when *Than* Armand dragged an oxcart across the yard with two missionaries in it, one reading a Bible and the other holding an open umbrella over his head. Another missionary ran alongside, stopped the cart, and then climbed up into it. Finally someone recognized the story of Philip from Acts, chapter 8. Later in the week the campers themselves acted out several stories. Peng watched intently on these occasions, reading the stories in his Bible at night. He was discovering many new things and was anxious to share them with his tribal friends at home. The people described in God's Word were becoming very real to him.

Several young people were converted that week. Although some of these were from Christian homes, they admitted they had never before personally received Jesus as Savior.

On Sunday evening the closing service was held outside on the grass between the buildings. Standing near a bright pressure lamp within the circle of young people, *Than* Hermann encouraged the campers to tell what God had done in their lives that week. At first there was no response, but then Peng's missionary friend Kathy began to tell what Jesus meant to her. Afterwards Anna told how she had become a Christian in Switzerland.

The growing darkness of the night seemed to press at their backs as the campers looked at one another timidly. It wasn't easy to speak in front of such a large group. Finally a Laotian girl stood and said she had decided to start having a daily quiet time of Bible reading and prayer when she got home from camp. Several other girls gave a similar testimony.

The local pastor led the campers in singing Gospel choruses as *Than* Hermann pumped up the pressure lamp, for the light had begun to weaken. Then a boy in the row behind Peng stood up and admitted his lukewarmness toward the Lord and asked for prayer. Some boys near him who had been joking and snickering all through the service were suddenly quiet.

Peng never forgot the final testimony. A tall, attractive girl named Malee said she was going to teach herself to read so she could go to Bible school someday. Peng had noticed that in class she had listened intently to the Bible lessons but had never opened her Bible. It was evidently because she couldn't read! He wondered if she would ever qualify to enter the Bible school. It would be hard to sit and study all day for months at a time if one couldn't read very well. He knew he couldn't do it, for he liked to be active, working in the fields and making things with his hands. But he would miss studying the Bible with the missionaries in Mong. They went at a pace he could follow. It was going to be very lonely if no one came to live in Mong and teach him in the coming months.

Peng felt very happy as he looked around at his many new friends, yet sad that Bible camp was almost over. He longed to stand up and tell what Jesus meant to him, but he felt unable to express his feelings in Laotian in front of all these people.

15

Paddy Field Test

A FEW WEEKS AFTER Youth Camp, Peng was playing Christian music on the phonograph in the field house when he heard running feet and excited voices outside. He jumped up and went out onto the porch. Two white men were running up the path . . .

"*Than* John!" he exclaimed. "You've come back! Praise God!"

John was equally excited. "It's so good to see you again, Peng. I've come to show *Than* Ron the way to your village. Our mission leaders have asked me to work in a village up on the mountain, but Ron's going to live in Mong now."

"That's wonderful news! Come inside and rest awhile," Peng invited. He had become good friends with Kathy's fiancé Ron during Youth Camp, but he was sorry that John and Dorothy would not be coming back to live near him.

"How is your wife, *Than* John? Is she well now?" he asked eagerly.

"Yes, her health is fine. And we have a son!" beamed John. "It was good to see our family and friends in America. But we were always thinking of you, and we asked everybody we met to pray for you every day!"

Peng was overwhelmed to think that so many

people he had never met were praying for him. "It was very lonely and difficult sometimes," he admitted. "But God has really helped me, and now Dee and Nuen are following Jesus too."

As they talked for several hours, John could see that Peng had learned much from the women missionaries and from the week at Youth Camp. In fact, his deep understanding of the Scriptures was astounding. He could read the Laotian Bible, and explain the way of salvation through Jesus quite clearly.

However, Peng admitted he had often failed God. He told John he was especially troubled because he hadn't been able to exorcise the offending spirit from his father's rice granary. Although the village priests had divined that it was the cause of a rash of sickness which had recently struck the village, even they had not been able to appease the spirit or remove it.

"Can you drive the demon out for me?" Peng asked John.

Somewhat nonplussed at this unusual request, John gulped and said, "Yes, I think so." He had never been taught how to deal with evil spirits, so he felt a little fearful of such a confrontation with the spirit world.

But they went out to the rice paddy, walked around the granary and asked what had been done. Then along with Peng and Ron, John simply bowed his head and prayed there in front of the granary, commanding in the name of Jesus that the demon vacate the premises and not cause any further trouble.

John learned how powerful that simple prayer of faith had been when Peng told him later that that particular spirit had never been heard from again. The villagers were grateful for this deliverance, but years afterward when their spirit priests were unable to contact that demon, this became an additional reason to persecute the Christians.

Peng had several questions and problems which he shared with John and Ron that evening after they returned from the rice granary. His greatest concern was for his parents.

"Why do they still not believe?" he asked. "They have seen God's power keep me safe from the evil spirits' anger. How long will it be before they trust in Jesus too?"

The men did their best to encourage him. They prayed together, claiming God's power to draw Samat and Suk to the Savior, realizing that Satan would fight hard to keep further inroads from being made into his territory.

One day Samat announced it was nearly time to make the traditional blood sacrifice to appease the spirit of the fields so they could begin the planting. Peng had thought much about this, and he spoke firmly. "I can't help you make fields this year, father. You give the spirits all the credit, but I know it was Jesus who gave us a good crop last year."

Samat frowned at him, feeling puzzled. What should he do with this son who had become so wilful? Families should cling together. The Taway way of life would surely be torn into unrecognizable pieces if everyone followed his own ideas. Any person who forgot his ancestors and their teachings would soon lose his identity and be swallowed up by the restless masses who lived only for physical satisfaction.

Surely his son would not go that far, Samat assured himself. A mystifying tranquillity and joy radiated from Peng, even though he had many strange ideas and preferred the foreigners' religion. It was amazing that the spirits had not been able to harm him since he had rejected their ways. Could it be that Jesus really was more powerful than the forest spirits?

Samat decided there was a way to find out. After all, Peng was a man now, 25 years old. Even though he was still unmarried, it was time he took on more responsibility.

"All right, son," Samat said finally. "I'll give you five rice fields to plant by yourself your own way. But I doubt that the spirit of the fields will give life to your rice if you don't make the proper offerings."

"Thank you, father!" Peng's eyes were wide with joy. "Jesus will give me a good crop. All life comes from Him."

With great excitement Peng surveyed his fields the next day. Now he could demonstrate God's power in a visible way no one could ignore!

He was busy repairing the paddy dikes the following week when Ron came to visit. Peng told him the good news.

"I want to dedicate these fields to Jesus. Can we hold a ceremony to ask Him to bless the rice I plant here?"

Ron thought fast. "We could walk around the edges of the fields singing praise to God and then pray, putting each field into His care."

The neighbors were puzzled when they heard Peng and the tall blond man singing in the fields that afternoon. They watched them march around each of Peng's paddies, then stop to bow their heads and pray to the Creator God. When Peng's friends noticed that he made no blood sacrifices to the evil spirits, they were sure he was headed for disaster.

Later that week the spirit priests performed their ceremonies to determine the most propitious time to plant the rice. For three days there was a *kalaam baan*.[1] No one was allowed to come and go from the village while the spirits were being consulted; loud feasting and drinking went on day and night.

Peng stayed in the field house while his parents and Ying went up to the *kalaam baan*. Fourteen-year-old Dee stayed with him. However, Sahn again yielded to pressure from his wife and in-laws. He joined in the ceremonies and feasting, although he still claimed to trust in Jesus. Even Nuen went to the festivities, but he later told Peng he was

---

[1] Literally, "forbidden village", a time when all outsiders are forbidden to enter the village lest they offend the evil spirits.

sorry he had gone. It was difficult for him to break away from the old habits.

When the *kalaam baan* was over, the people came down to the fields. Peng and Dee watched from the porch of the little field house as their neighbors sprinkled the blood of a chicken on the ground and put up fetishes of bamboo and chicken feathers to guard the rice against harm.

Peng's heart ached for all the Taway who lived in bondage to the evil spirits. Many times he had told his neighbors there was deliverance only through the blood of Jesus, but they refused to listen. He lay awake that night praying that soon the veil of darkness would be lifted from their hearts.

After several heavy rains had soaked the ground, Peng sharpened his hoe and broke the ground. His father might have let him use one of the family buffaloes, but he decided not to ask. He was quite handy with a hoe, and the hours passed quickly as he worked. After the rains had again flooded the fields later that week, he removed the plug from the dikes and let the water out. Taking rice seed which had been soaking in a pot, he sowed it over the mud in one of his fields. A few days later when the sprouts had come up he sealed the dikes again and let the rain fill the paddy.

When the seedlings were about eight inches tall Peng pulled them up gently, slapping the wet roots against his bare feet to knock off the mud and muck. Gathering these into bunches, he wrapped a vine tightly around the roots and attached them to the ends of his shoulder pole. He carried the bundles into the other paddies and laid them out neatly, then took them apart and planted each seedling one by one in the deep mud, spacing them carefully about nine inches apart so they would have room to grow.

While working in the muddy fields, he wore his black-and-white plaid bathing cloth wrapped around his waist, the skirt pulled between his legs and tucked up in the back, so that it was almost as if he was wearing a pair of shorts. This gave him freedom of movement and was easier to wash and dry than his trousers. The hot, exhausting work in the fields didn't bother Peng; he had done it since he was a child, and he rather enjoyed strenuous physical labor.

Sometimes a gentle rain fell, cooling the air, but after the sun came out again the weather was usually more humid than before. No one stopped even when the rain became heavy. The rice had to be transplanted quickly.

Peng paused to straighten his back. He could see his mother and sister helping Samat in a paddy nearby. They had old towels wrapped around their heads to keep the perspiration out of their eyes. Even his father had a cloth turban on his head, as he himself did. In every field women and children were working beside their menfolk.

Peng knew why his mother and sister didn't help him; they were apprehensive about working in paddies not protected by the spirits. But he was content to care for his fields by himself. He was going to demonstrate the power of Jesus so his village would never forget it!

As they helped Samat transplant the seedlings, Suk and Ying discussed Peng's strange behavior.

"He'll soon be sorry," Suk declared. "The spirit of the fields will not allow his rice to grow."

"I hope the spirits will not be so angry that they will harm him," Ying said. She felt her brother was doing a very dangerous thing.

But Peng's rice grew as well as anyone's. He guarded his fields carefully to be sure that crabs and other predators did not get in. When the heavy monsoon rains came he spent many hours each day checking and strengthening the dikes that held in the water.

Then the rains stopped for several weeks, and the rice stalks began to wither under the burning sun. The people searched the sky anxiously for signs of rain. They diverted water from the river into their paddies, but they knew this could be only a temporary solution. If the drought continued the river would eventually become too low to be of much help.

Peng remained calm, assured that God would not forget the fields placed in His care. He carried buckets of water to his paddies and constantly claimed God's protection. Strangely, his rice stayed green although other fields began to turn brown.

There were angry mutterings in many homes. Heng said to his neighbors, "The spirits are punishing us for allowing Peng to worship the foreign god. We must force him to make an offering to appease their anger."

Without inviting Samat to join them, the men discussed the situation with the village headman and the other spirit priests. They decided to confront Peng in the morning.

But that night the rains finally came, a downpour that washed out many dikes and rice plants. When the people repaired the damage the next day they saw that Peng's fields had not been harmed. Why had the evil spirits punished them instead of him? Or had his God sent this disaster? They decided to say nothing to Peng, but they watched him closely. Perhaps he had put a curse on their paddies.

It was now the height of the monsoon season, and the roads were sometimes impassable. In any case, Peng was so busy in his fields that he found it difficult to go into Mong regularly, so he invited Ron to stay with him for a few weeks.

Ron eagerly accepted the invitation. He found it very interesting living in the field house where he could observe the Taway customs and begin to learn their language. He also enjoyed helping Peng in the fields. They became very close friends and often sang as they worked together.

The village at the foot of the mountains fascinated Ron with its tall wooden houses scattered among the boulders and palm trees. He admired the Taway system of bamboo pipes which brought fresh spring water down from above. But he didn't often go up to Ban Dao, because the people there would rarely speak to him. When he met them down in their paddy fields, however, they would usually talk freely and sometimes even invite him into their field houses, although few showed any interest in the Gospel.

Peng often took Ron to visit the potters' village where Nuen and Vahn lived. The people who made the earthen jars used in Taway homes were required to live in a separate village near the river. Sometimes the women went there to have their babies, because when a child was born inside the main village the mother was not allowed to leave for three months. In the potters' village the rules were more relaxed. Peng's Uncle Vahn liked living there because, although he was crippled, he was allowed to come and go as he wished.

The potters' kilns were built deep in the ground. Normally they were considered taboo or *kalaam* for anyone who didn't work in them, but after Nuen became a Christian he decided this didn't matter, and one day he allowed Ron to go down inside them and look around.

One evening Samat brought home a cobra for supper. He hadn't happened to have a gun or crossbow with him in the forest when he saw the snake, so he had killed it with a large stick. Peng said it would be delicious, so Ron bravely tasted the meat after Suk had cooked it. Not bad, he thought, although he still preferred chicken or fish. Samat couldn't eat the snake meat himself. Pork was also forbidden to him because of his vows to serve as a spirit priest.

Often they had boiled or fried eggs with their rice instead of meat. Sometimes Peng would shoot a chicken during the day with his crossbow, but usually he would catch one when it came to roost under the house at dusk and would put it in a basket to be killed and prepared the next day. His mother would chop the meat into small pieces and stew it with onions and herbs.

Other days the family ate monkey meat, snail, crabs or fish which they caught in their ponds during the rainy season. Chunks of pumpkin or pieces of bamboo or lemon grass gave these *kengs* a delicious flavor, whatever the meat was. For their morning meal they usually had just rice, salt, and roasted hot peppers, and sometimes also a hard-boiled egg.

Frequently Peng took time off to go with Ron to preach in nearby villages. One day they rode Ron's little Honda 50cc. motorbike south to Ban Tee. Many bridges along the road had been blown up in the war, so they had to ford the streams on foot and pull the motorbike up steep river banks.

They left the bike out in the forest near the edge of a rice field and walked the last kilometer to the village. The people were somewhat unfriendly, but eventually a small crowd gathered to listen to them explain the Gospel message, using several colorful posters they had brought along.

Suddenly they heard the rumble of mortar fire as big army guns attacked rebel hide-outs in the forest nearby. Peng realized the shots were landing just beyond where they had parked the motor-bike!

Not wanting to risk getting trapped there overnight, they left immediately. As they raced back across the paddy fields, exposed to the gunfire, they were suddenly drenched by a cloudburst. They could scarcely see a hundred feet ahead through the rain.

"God was good to send us that cover just when we needed it!" Ron gasped breathlessly as they ducked into the woods, safe at last. Water trickled off their wet hair into their eyes, and the posters they had brought were ruined, but they were glad to be alive.

"The army must think some of the rebels are hiding near the village," Peng said, climbing onto the bike behind Ron. "They're probably right. I saw several men who looked as if they might have been 'forest people' working with the Pathet Lao."[2]

A chill ran down Ron's back as he realized they could easily have been captured by the enemy. Even now the Laotian army might shoot at them, mistaking them for rebels. He was grateful the heavy rain was still falling, even though it made the road muddy and difficult to travel.

After they had ridden about five kilometers the rain suddenly stopped. They reached the stream a few minutes later.

---

[2] The Pathet Lao faction had been given representation in the government in 1958, but they continued to work in conjunction with the North Vietnamese troops who had invaded Laos. Living in secret hide-outs from which they would attack villages, they were often called "forest people."

"Praise the Lord! It's not flooded!" Ron shouted. They were able to cross the streams and gullies easily all the way home, and they finally reached Ban Dao safely.

This was the last time they visited that area, for the Ho Chi Minh trail was thought to pass only a few kilometers south of Ban Tee, and the authorities refused to give them permission to travel there again.

Usually the fighting was far away from Peng's village, and he tried not to think about it. The Taway people didn't like to discuss the war that was tearing their country apart, for most of them were loyal to the Royal Laotian government. However, Peng knew that in every tribe a small group was willing to align with either side if only they would be left alone to live their lives in peace.

Soon Ron moved back to Mong, but a short while later he returned to Ban Dao one morning with three strangers. Peng noticed the men were rather dark-complexioned, yet not as dark as Laotians, and their eyes were slanted, shaped like the nuts he sometimes picked on the side of the mountain. Many of the Taway people gathered to stare at the visitors, and Peng heard someone murmur that yellow-skinned foreigners like these had occupied Laos during the great war. He himself had a vague memory of seeing such soldiers when he was a small child.

"These men are from Japan," Ron said, introducing each one by name. "They've come to spend a year in Laos helping us take God's Word to those who have never heard it."

The Taway had never seen a Christian Japanese or met anyone from that race who had come on a peaceful mission, but they knew many people in Laos had suffered when the Japanese had occupied their country. They listened eagerly, impressed that these men were different because of their faith in Jesus.

The Japanese Christians had been in Laos only a short time and had not yet learned much of the language. They spoke English, and Ron put their words into Laotian as they greeted the people and gave their testimonies. Peng translated each sentence into the Taway language for the group of curious neighbors who gathered to watch the odd-looking foreigners.

For several weeks Ron traveled with the Japanese men, taking them to many villages in the area. Several times Peng went along to help interpret. Although many tribal villages received them politely, there were no new converts. A few people did express a desire to follow the Jesus way, but they wanted to wait until the village headman and others also believed.

"We do everything together," a tribal man explained. "One person cannot be different from the rest of the tribe. We have an old proverb that says one person can't accomplish anything by himself." When told that Peng had stood alone for many months and now others were joining him, the elderly man was visibly impressed but still unwilling to follow his example.

When Peng went into Mong a few weeks later Ron told him the Japanese Christians had moved on to another province.

"They want to proclaim the good news about Jesus in every village they can reach during the months they are in Laos," Ron explained. "They don't feel called to stay and teach the believers, but they want to sow God's Word in many hearts and show that it can change even Japanese lives."

Although there was still much to do in the fields, Peng continued to go out witnessing with Ron wherever possible, returning several times to each village. Some people were eager to be delivered from the power of the evil spirits, but no one was willing to take the first step.

"We all depend on each other," one man said. "The boat needs the water; the tiger finds refuge in the forest. Nobody can walk alone and survive."

On the way home Ron told Peng, "These people are blinded by Satan. Their hearts are like hard ground, but we must continue to sow the Word of God, for some day it will bear fruit."

That afternoon as they emerged from the forest near Peng's village, they heard men shouting in the distance and saw people running through the rice fields, waving their arms frantically.

"The pigs are loose in the fields!" a man called to them. "Come and help us catch them!"

Ron and Peng joined in the wild chase, and finally all the pigs were put back into their pens.

Many precious rice stalks had been trampled down, but when Peng checked his fields he found they were among the few that had escaped any damage.

Some of the people were impressed by the supernatural power that seemed to protect him, but others became resentful.

"Peng thinks he is better than we are, but someday we'll make him sorry he left the ways of our forefathers," Heng said to his neighbors. His wife Lansee shuddered when she heard this. Something terrible was certain to happen to Peng. She was glad she had not married him.

16

Hope Deferred

WHEN PENG HARVESTED his rice in November, his heart was full of praise. God had given him an abundant crop.

"Now you know it is safe to follow Jesus," he told his parents. "God protected my rice from the drought, the floods, and even from the pigs."

Samat admitted that Jesus appeared to be more powerful than the evil spirits. He had never seen so much rice harvested from five small paddies, but he still refused to enter the Jesus religion.

"I am an old man. It's too late for me to learn new ways," he said.

Peng couldn't understand why his parents wouldn't trust in Jesus. He knew there was power in prayer, for God had protected his rice fields. Why didn't God answer his prayers for his parents' salvation?

For several months now he had been playing the new Taway records made by David Henriksen the previous year. Even his father and mother enjoyed hearing them. Peng found much comfort in the messages about the resurrection and Jesus calming the storm. He had thought surely the record telling about the broad road to hell and the one about Noah and the flood would cause many of his people to realize the danger of rejecting Jesus.

But there were no more conversions. In fact, things became worse. Bek, Lam, and Pak were no longer friendly, and the young people stopped coming to hear the records. Once Peng went to Heng's house to tell him about Jesus, but neither Heng nor Lansee would invite him in or listen to him.

Then Nuen became very sick. Afraid to die, he turned to the spirit priests for guidance and made a sacrifice appeasing the demons, yet he failed to improve. Peng tried to persuade him to call upon Jesus for help, but he refused, and after about ten days he died.

Peng wished he could talk things over with Ron, but he had left Mong near the end of September, seriously ill with hepatitis. Later Ron wrote saying he had recovered but that he and Kathy were going home to America to be married. They would not be returning to live in Mong until January.

In the meantime Peng felt very much alone. Since Nuen had died, Dee had stopped coming over to study and pray with him. Sahn was still clinging to the old ways. He had a little son now and was afraid for the child's safety.

"When my son is old enough to believe in Jesus, my whole family will follow the Jesus way together," he had said. Although Peng had tried to reassure him that Jesus could protect them now, Sahn wouldn't listen.

As the dry season turned colder, Peng recalled that Christians set aside a certain day in December to remember Christ's coming into the world. Last year he had taken Sahn with him to celebrate this occasion with the women missionaries in Mong, but now there was no one there, and he didn't even know which day was Christmas. He felt very discouraged. Although he had followed Jesus faithfully for nearly two years, he was still very alone. He began to spend more time in prayer and found that this would usually brighten his outlook on life. "The missionaries cannot always be here with me," he reasoned, "so I must learn to depend more upon God. Jesus has promised that whatever happens, He will never leave me nor forsake me, and that is all that matters."

Finally in January Ron and Kathy Smith arrived back in Mong, and the lonely months were over. Once the harvest was in, Peng visited them frequently. He would sit with his Bible open, listening to them hour after hour. Their voices would tire long before his spiritual thirst was quenched. Occasionally Dee would go into town with him, but he didn't have the same eagerness to learn.

One Sunday Ron and Kathy rode their bikes out to visit Peng at the garden house. They had arranged to hold a meeting there so that Uncle Vahn could attend. He was not yet a believer, but he was always eager to hear more about Jesus.

Peng looked completely dejected when he arrived. "I'm alone again," he said. "The village council met last week and threatened to fine us for violating the tribal customs. Dee gave in and made a spirit sacrifice."

Kathy shook her head sadly. "I guess Dee's too young to be able to stand against the whole village. He's only fourteen, isn't he?"

"Yes, and being an orphan makes it hard for him. But there's really nothing they can do to us if we stand firm."

Before the meeting started, Dee himself appeared in the doorway. He handed his New Testament to Ron.

"I can't keep this," he said. "I have to follow the ancestor spirits now. There's no one else in my family to do it." Dee's mother had been a spirit priest, and his aunt and uncle expected him to carry on the traditions of the family.

Nothing Ron said would change Dee's mind. He refused to attend the Bible study but waited outside in the yard, and when the meeting was over he ate dinner with them. He didn't seem bitter, just sad. Afterwards he sat a short distance from the house playing the Gospel records while the others talked.

"Sometimes I feel I can't go on alone," Peng said, glancing at Ron to see if he understood. "But last night God comforted me through these words." He opened his Bible to Psalm 86 and read several verses:

"In the day of my trouble I will call upon You, for You will answer me. Among the gods there is none like You, O Lord; nor are there any works like Your works. All nations whom You have made shall come and worship before You, O Lord, and shall glorify Your name."

He looked up with a bright smile. "That means someday even the Taway people will worship the Lord, doesn't it? I hope that time comes soon. I'm getting tired of waiting."

"You could go to Bible School in Savannakhet so you'll be ready to teach your people when they do believe in Jesus," Ron suggested. "The spring semester starts in a few weeks."

Peng looked thoughtful. "Maybe I should do that. I could sell some of my rice to pay for the bus fare and other expenses." But when he considered it later he decided he probably couldn't read well enough. It would be embarrassing if he couldn't keep up with the other students. He didn't really want to go to Bible School that spring anyway, for he was sure his parents would trust in Jesus soon if he continued to witness to them. He tried to be a good son, helping the family in every way possible. With his hoe he cleared away the weeds that were always growing up around the house. The encroaching jungle had to be fought continually lest it swallow the village.

Peng gave his parents most of the rice harvested from his five paddy fields. Now their granaries were overflowing, and they had extra rice to trade for things they needed. Suk noticed that several neighbors had started using mattresses, and she decided to make some for her family. She arranged for the casings to be sewed together by a friend in Ban Dao who had a treadle sewing machine. Special offerings to appease the spirits had made the machine acceptable, even in the main village, though so many other modern things were forbidden. Much money could be earned with a sewing machine, for people were always needing new shorts, shirts or blouses. Two families in Ban Dao had them now, and had learned to use them and keep them in good repair. They bought the cloth for their work from the Laotians or Huay people, because the Taway looms were too narrow to weave anything except their women's skirts and the men's loincloths.

Suk brought the mattress casings home one afternoon, and Peng helped her stuff them. Having planted their own kapok trees in the village, they had plenty of stuffing. Several weeks earlier the pods had been pulled off the trees and left to dry in the sun. Finally bursting open, they had spilled out piles of soft, cottony material dotted with tiny black seeds. Peng and Ying had helped Suk with the tedious job of removing these. Kapok was soft and durable, ideal for stuffing mattresses and pillows, and whenever he worked with it, Peng marveled at God's wisdom and love in creating such a useful tree.

Ying also helped stuff the mattresses, and afterward she sewed the ends together with the cotton thread she had spun herself. Like the Laotians, Taway grew some cotton, and she had learned at an early age to spin thread and make her own dye. However, since the war had spread from Vietnam into Laos, many women no longer had time to spin thread and weave colorful skirts, for they had to work in the fields in place of their husbands and sons who had joined the Laotian army and gone off to fight.

Peng was glad the rice from his field made it possible for his parents to have a few comforts. Since their field hut was quite small, useful only when they camped out during the planting season or harvest time, Samat began to build a larger house at the edge of his paddy fields. He planned to keep the mattresses there, and also an old bicycle he had recently bought. When the missionaries came to visit, there would be more room for them and for the crowd that sometimes gathered.

Peng was pleased that his father didn't seem to cling to tradition as rigidly as in the past. "Perhaps soon he will trust in Jesus," he thought.

But at the moment Samat was more interested in accumulating possessions than in listening to the Gospel. He was hurrying to finish his new house before the dry season ended. Peng went into the forest with him to hunt for the large bamboo that was used for the floors and walls, and they would work together until late each evening. Suk and Ying gathered long grasses for the thatch, tying them into neat bundles ready to be assembled on the roof.

Peng looked forward to Sundays when he usually went into town to study the Bible with Ron and Kathy, for he always had new questions that had arisen during his daily reading at home during the week. Often he would stay overnight with the missionaries, and they would go out preaching on Monday. Actually, he felt closer in spirit to the foreigners than to his own family.

Ron had bad news for him one Sunday. He told him, "This week I received a letter from the missionaries in Solane saying that the three Japanese Christians have been captured by the rebel army. No one knows if they are still alive."

Suddenly the risks of preaching the Gospel in Laos became more real than ever before to Ron and Kathy, and also to Peng. He was amazed that they were willing to remain in Mong when they knew their own lives could be in danger at any time.

"I'll take more precautions when going out into the countryside, and I won't stay in any village overnight," Ron said. "The local authorities would warn us to leave if it became too dangerous here. But I don't think the Lord wants us to leave Mong yet."

The rainy season began, and Peng planted his fields again. He was still urging his father to trust in Jesus, but Samat said he wasn't interested in the foreign religion.

"I've promised to serve the spirits all my life. They will kill me if I don't continue to appease them."

Peng was very disappointed. The Gospel recordings in the Taway language explained the way of salvation so clearly that no one could possibly misunderstand. His father had also seen how Jesus had protected his rice crop the previous year. Why didn't he want to be free from the spirits? Peng's heart became hard and bitter whenever he thought of his father. He found it hard to pray, and he had no joy. Finally he went to Ron for advice.

"Your father is blinded by Satan. You must continue to love him and pray for him," Ron said. "But you must love Jesus more than your parents." He showed Peng some verses in Matthew chapter ten: "A man's foes shall be those of his own household. He who loves father or mother more than me is not worthy of me; and he who loves son or daughter more than me is not worthy of me. And he who does not take his cross and follow after me is not worthy of me."

Peng realized he had to decide whether he would go on with Jesus or turn back to please his parents. He knew he would go on. Jesus had given him peace of heart and freedom from the fear of death, and there was nothing in the old life to draw him back. He prayed, "Lord, even if I have to leave my parents and become like an orphan, I will always follow you."

God helped him to have more patience with his father, but still Samat's attitude did not change. Finally Peng decided to go to Bible School. He realized he needed more training in order to win his people to Jesus. He would obey God and leave his parents in God's hands.

When he went into town to tell Ron, he found him living alone. Kathy had gone ahead into Thailand to await the birth of her first child at the mission hospital there.

"Bible School started a week ago," Ron said. "But it's probably not too late to get in. You can travel with me when I go to Solane at the end of the week."

Ron helped him get a travel pass, and they left on an army plane a few days later. They separated in Solane, where Ron crossed the border into Thailand, anxious to reach the hospital before the baby was born. Peng rode a bus to Savannakhet, somewhat apprehensive about the new experience ahead of him, but determined to learn how to win his tribe to Jesus.

17

Bible School

WHEN PENG ENTERED the mission compound in Savannakhet, he saw the tall Swiss missionary, *Than* Armand, working on his red pickup truck in the shade near the gate. The missionary looked up and quickly recognized him in his neat white shirt, and dark trousers.

"Peng! *Sambai baw*! What brings you to Savannakhet?" he called.

"I've come to attend the Bible School," Peng said, walking over to him.

"Our classes started two weeks ago, but I guess we could let you in. You'll soon catch up." Armand remembered Peng well from Youth Camp the year before, and knew he had an intensity of purpose that would compensate for his late arrival and lack of previous education.

Putting his tools aside, he took Peng to the boys' dorms over behind the Lao chapel. Inside one room a slender young man was sitting on the floor studying. When he saw Peng enter he jumped up excitedly.

"*Sambai baw*, Peng! What are you doing here?"

Peng's nervousness fell away and he smiled broadly. "I've come to attend Bible School," he answered, recognizing Danee, whom he had met at Youth Camp. Son of the leading church elder in

Khone, Danee was quiet and shy like himself; with him around he wouldn't feel lonely.

"Peng can sleep next to you, Danee," Armand said. "Since you seem to be good friends already, I'll get back to working on my truck."

Peng put down his small bundle of clothes wrapped in a blanket. He looked around him and saw three mats on the floor with an empty space next to where Danee had been sitting.

"Kee sleeps in here, too," Danee said. "He'll be glad to see you again. He and the other boys are down at the river bathing. Let's go and join them!"

At supper time Peng discovered there were nine girls attending the Bible School that semester, and seven boys beside himself. Usually the boys and girls ate separately, but that evening everyone was eating together at *Than* Armand's house on the verandah upstairs. Peng and Kee helped spread some bamboo mats on the floor, one row for the boys and one row for the girls.

Several missionaries came to eat with the students. Peng saw Rosemary, who used to live in Mong, carrying in a bowl of *keng* and a saucer of dried chili peppers mixed with fish sauce. When she saw him she almost spilled the food in her excitement. "Peng!" she cried with a big smile. His heart felt warm with happiness to see her again. She controlled her enthusiasm and put the dishes down carefully on a mat, then greeted him politely in the Laotian manner with her head bowed over her hands held palm-to-palm under her chin.

"*Sambai baw*! Have you come to study with us?" she asked.

Peng flashed a bright smile to her as he bobbed his head in answer. "*Sambai dee, Nang*[1] Put," he said, using her Laotian name. "Yes, I've finally come to Bible School."

The next morning after chapel he went with Danee and Kee to his first class, New Testament Introduction. Peng followed slowly in his Bible as Rosemary read the lesson in Luke. The verses were unfamiliar to him and seemed hard to understand. After discussing the text the teacher wrote five questions on the chalkboard.

"Your homework today is to write out answers to these questions," she said. She was trying to teach them to analyze the Scriptures and think things through for themselves rather than learn everything by memory as they usually did in public school.

Quickly the students copied the questions and some had begun to write out their answers when the gong sounded for the end of the period. She dismissed them, and there was a rustle of books and sandaled feet as the young people hurried out to their next class.

Peng was still writing laboriously, his short black hair tousled and his square jaw set with determination as he struggled to reproduce the Laotian words in his notebook.

---

[1] *Nang* is a title of respect for an unmarried woman.

"You can finish copying the questions later from Danee's paper," Rosemary told him kindly. "Pretty soon you'll be able to write as quickly as the others. I'm so happy you've come."

By the end of his first week Peng was becoming used to the busy schedule, although he thought it strange that at the close of each hour he had to hurry to another classroom to be taught by a different teacher. The foreign teachers had some odd ways, but he found their lessons interesting.

Soon he decided that his favorite class was Old Testament Survey. He greatly admired Abraham, Joseph and Moses, and aimed to follow their examples, even though it seemed unlikely he himself could ever become a leader, since he felt he had failed miserably to persuade his tribe to trust in the living God.

Once a week the five first-year students met with the rest of the school to study church history, also taught by Rosemary. These lessons were quite difficult. Peng learned that hundreds of years ago many believers in Jesus had suffered and even died for their faith. Their names were strange and hard to remember, and he couldn't comprehend exactly where they had lived even though the teacher pointed out the countries on a large map. But knowing that so many people had suffered for their faith in Jesus made Peng determined that he also would stand firm, whatever the cost.

He soon became close friends with a second-year student named Meekay. They often studied their church history lesson together, discussing what they would do if the Laotian government should begin to persecute Christians. Peng hoped that he would have the strength to stand true to Christ even if it cost his life.

Each student in the Bible School was responsible for doing his own laundry. The girls scrubbed their clothes in buckets or large washpans outside their dormitory under the shade of the trees, using the chunks of yellow soap that the missionaries had bought at the market for them. Like the other boys, Peng usually washed his clothes when he went down to the river to swim and bathe, later hanging his shirt and pants out to dry on a line or a fence back at the missionary compound. He always enjoyed his afternoon swim in the river.

The girls sometimes went to the river, but they usually bathed in the shower room behind the mission house. Peng heard that water was pumped from the cistern to the roof of the small building so that by just turning a faucet one could make the water come out through a pipe overhead.

Although the boys didn't have a shower, they had their own toilet facilities in a small room behind their dorm. At home in their villages they just went out in the forest, but of course this was not possible in town. The missionaries tried to make life comfortable for the students, but they wanted to keep things simple so that the young people would adjust easily to life back in the villages.

There were no tables or chairs in the dorm rooms, but Peng didn't mind sitting on his mat to study. However, every evening a study period was held in the classrooms so the students could sit at a table to write out their homework, supervised by one of the missionaries. Peng was continually fascinated by the switch that turned on the lights, but sometimes the power was low and the bulb was so dim it was useless. Then the missionaries would bring in a pressure lamp which gave out a very bright light, although it was noisy and made the room hot.

A mosquito net hung above each mat in the dormitories. Surprised to hear that malaria and dengue fever were transmitted by mosquitoes, Peng learned to tuck the net in carefully under the edges of his mat before he went to sleep at night. He felt he was living in great luxury and sometimes longed for the simple ways of his village.

Everyone took turns doing the marketing and cooking the meals, even the boys. The girls often teased them about who could cook the best, but they took it with good humor. A boy always went along to carry the heavy baskets when a girl was doing the marketing, and by observing carefully they all learned how to pick out the best produce and bargain for a good price.

One morning, it was Peng and Danee's turn to go to market. They had to get up very early to reach the market place before the best foods were sold out, and to get back to the school in time for breakfast. Peng enjoyed being outside at dawn as the dark sky faded into a pink glow. The streets were thronged with people from the countryside bringing baskets of produce to sell. Watching the rays of the rising sun paint everything with a special vibrancy and new life, Peng felt happy and full of energy.

He thought the crowded market was a cheerful, colorful place. The women wore bright flowered skirts and many carried Chinese parasols to shield themselves from the hot sun. People bargained noisily over the wares, and live chickens squawked inside bamboo cages. All kinds of fruit and vegetables were spread out in long rows on the ground, some under the open sky and others under a large roof that had been built that year with American aid. Many people had their wares arranged neatly on large pieces of bright red or green plastic; others spread them out on the cement or on large banana leaves.

Recently the Lao money had been devalued again. Peng didn't know if it was because of the war or whether the inflation was caused by so many foreigners coming into Laos. The American civilians who had come to help with government services seemed to have unlimited money to rent the best houses in town, and prices were continually rising. It now took 400 *kip* instead of only 100 to equal an American dollar. Meat was especially expensive and scarce, since there were so many foreigners wanting to buy it. Passing the meat stall Peng saw a frantic mob shouting and pushing at one another. He was glad he didn't have to get in line. The students couldn't afford to eat beef or pork unless a Christian in a nearby village slaughtered an animal and brought them some meat.

Danee and Peng bought some red and green chili peppers, two hands of bananas and a live chicken. They had to bargain for each item to get the best possible price; the seller expected this and it was like a game to see who would win. Danee picked out a large papaya and managed to buy it for only twenty *kip*.

The girls had asked them also to get some green onions and lemon grass for seasoning. As Peng followed Danee slowly through the crowd hunting for these items he saw potatoes, carrots, lettuce, corn and cabbage which he knew were grown up in the mountains where the air was cooler than in the hot lowlands. He had heard these strange foods were popular with the Americans, Vietnamese and Chinese, but the students weren't accustomed to eating them.

Suddenly he jabbed Danee in the back with his fist. "What's that?" he asked, pointing to the right with his chin.

"That big round fruit is a watermelon," Danee said. "I think those little red berries are called strawberries. The missionary in Khone used to grow some in her garden. I tasted them once, but they're nothing special."

They couldn't find any onions or lemon grass for a good price, so they bought a tomato. The girls could use it with garlic for seasoning.

Walking home, they passed the bakery where a Vietnamese family made loaves of French bread to sell. Fresh bread had a pleasant smell, Peng thought. But he had found the taste too bland, and preferred rice. Each student brought some money and a large bag of rice to school. This was shared equally and must be made to last for the ten-week semester, although the missionaries and the Laotian church also contributed some money and food. Actually the meals were better than Peng had at home, although he sometimes missed the shrimp and tiny fish they caught in the ponds near his village.

They heard the loud blare of a radio as they passed a large Chinese home, a white stucco house surrounded by high walls. Peng was sure those people must be quite wealthy. He had never owned a radio, but more people were buying them all the time. Sometimes the students listened to Christian broadcasts in Laotian on the missionary's radio in the evenings. Laotian Christians worked with the missionaries every week to record these programs on tapes which were mailed to the Philippines and then transmitted back to Laos over the airwaves. Already some villages in the interior had radios and could hear the Gospel in this way.

Often Peng awakened early before dawn and went outside to pray under the trees where he wouldn't disturb the other boys. He prayed daily for his parents, his sisters, his brother Khap and for the missionaries who had brought him the Gospel, mentioning each by name and not forgetting the Japanese Christians who had been captured by the rebel army. They still had not been released, and he was concerned that their lives be spared.

Several afternoons each week the students went out witnessing, holding open air meetings in the villages nearby, sometimes passing out tracts in the Chinese or Vietnamese parts of town. They either went with a missionary or with their Lao teacher Souban, who was a captain in the Laotian army, very highly respected by everyone. He had a bold and fearless witness in spite of his prominent position in a country where nearly everyone else was Buddhist. Sometimes he preached in the Laotian chapel on Sunday mornings. Observing Captain Souban's zeal and love for souls, Peng hoped to become like him.

Each morning after breakfast the students and teachers met together for a chapel service before classes began. Following Laotian custom, the boys and girls sat on opposite sides of the small room. The students would report on the witnessing done the previous day, and sometimes one of the more advanced students gave a short devotional talk. Other mornings *Than* Armand would bring a Bible message, or a student would tell how he had found Christ as Savior. Many of the young people had grown up in Christian homes, but one girl came from a village that had just been evangelized earlier that year.

Armand Heiniger announced in chapel one morning that at last the Japanese missionaries had been released unharmed and had returned to their homeland. During the time of prayer and praise that followed, Peng's heart overflowed with joy at this answer to prayer. Surely, he thought, God is also able to save my parents. He wrote them frequently, but weeks often went by with no letter from home. Samat and Suk couldn't write, and Peng knew it was difficult for his parents to find someone who could read his letters to them and write an answer, so he tried to be patient.

Early one morning before chapel he made a little sign requesting prayer for his parents and propped it up on the pulpit. Touched by Peng's concern for his family, the students and missionaries often mentioned Samat and Suk in their prayers after that.

Peng enjoyed playing dodgeball and relay games in the evenings before it grew dark. Occasionally the missionaries came to play volleyball at the mission compound, and some students learned to play with them. But Peng preferred to sit and watch. This was a good time to talk to the girls who were also watching the games.

He became good friends with a tall, attractive Laotian girl named Malee. He remembered her from youth camp, and he was impressed with her testimony given at chapel one day. Her family were the only Christians in their village, although church services had been held in her home as long as she could remember, and her parents had witnessed faithfully to their neighbors. Her younger brothers and sisters had gone to school, but as was customary for the eldest daughter in a family, she had always had to stay home to care for the toddlers and help with the cooking and other work.

At youth camp last year when she was seventeen, Malee had decided to teach herself to read so she could go to Bible School. So in the evenings after her chores were done she had begun to study the schoolbooks brought home by her brothers and sisters. They had helped her all they could, and last spring she had finally been able to enter the Bible School. Although she was now a second-year student, reading and writing were still difficult for her. Her cousin, a very bright third-year student, taught two of Peng's classes, Old Testament Survey and the Life of Christ.

Peng admired Malee and some of the other Bible School girls, but he tried not to get emotionally involved with any of them, for he knew that even among the Christians very few Laotians married tribal people. He would often lie awake at night, struggling to give up his dream of having a wife and children someday. He did want to put God's work first, but it was difficult when he was feeling so lonely. He was about five years older than the other students, and nearly everyone else was Laotian, although there was a tribal boy named Sep in his class. Sep was the youngest of the entire student body, but he was extremely intelligent and quick with his lessons. Peng was embarrassed to be so slow at times, but Malee encouraged him to persevere.

"I know how you feel," she said. "I have trouble keeping up with Sone in my class." Sone was a tribal girl who was part Chinese, and quite a bit younger than Malee. Peng was surprised that everyone got along so well together in spite of their differences in background and their varying levels of education.

He managed to pass his mid-term exams although his grades were low. Kee failed several classes, but he just laughed about it. "I've got better things to do than study," he said. He dropped out of school and soon Peng heard that he had joined the army.

Returning from a swim in the river one afternoon, Peng was amazed to find his brother Khap waiting for him outside the dormitory. He was so glad to see him, he gave him a quick hug as he had seen the missionaries do to one another. Khap looked surprised but hugged him back.

"Dee came to see me in Solane," he said, motioning toward the young boy standing shyly near the fence. "He wanted to find you. Since I was driving a truck up here this week, I decided to bring him along." Khap was still working as a driver for USAID.

Dee told Peng he was sorry he had turned away from the Lord Jesus. When he asked if he could enrol in the Bible School, Armand counseled with him and decided to let him stay although the semester was nearly half over. Obviously the boy didn't have a real home and needed Christian fellowship and grounding in the Scriptures.

Peng had a long talk with his brother, and finally Khap decided he would enter the Jesus way. "I know I'm a sinner," he admitted. "I need a new heart. Money and friends and adventure don't really satisfy." Peng wept with joy as his brother prayed, confessing his sins and asking Jesus into his heart.

Khap stayed overnight and went to church with Peng the next day. Gregarious by nature, he enjoyed meeting the Laotian Christians as they gathered at the chapel. After the sermon he went to the front of the room and gave his testimony with enthusiasm, declaring he was turning away from all spirit worship. Dee also said a few words, although more timidly. They were both baptized in the Mekong River that afternoon.

Khap then returned to his job in Solane, but he wrote to Peng frequently and it was soon evident he was reading his Bible, attending church and growing spiritually.

In mid-October Ron and Kathy Smith returned from Thailand with their little son Steve. John and Dorothy Davis and another missionary family also returned on the same train with newborn babies. Peng and the other students dutifully admired the three infants, but privately thought they looked strange, being so pale and nearly bald. Laotian and tribal infants nearly always had thick dark hair at birth.

In class one day as Rosemary was teaching the first-year students from the book of Acts, she discussed the coming of the Holy Spirit on the day of Pentecost.

"What does it mean to be filled with the Spirit?" she asked.

For a moment the class was silent, and the students looked at one another uncertainly. "Have you ever known anyone filled with the Spirit?" she probed.

Danee nodded his head. "Yes! Peng is filled with the Spirit. I wish I had God's love and power flowing through me like he does."

Peng was embarrassed. Danee's father was a church elder. Nearly all the other students had grown up in Christian homes and knew much more about God than he did, but they seemed to be casual about it, often not applying God's promises to themselves personally.

Finally the school term was over. Peng's grades were not high, but he managed to pass every test. A few weeks earlier the missionaries had announced that after school was out they would take a group of students to evangelize the hill tribes in the interior. Peng decided to go with them. He dreaded returning to the ridicule, suspicion and loneliness of his home village. It seemed better to go where people were eager to hear the Gospel. He prayed daily for his parents, but he still found it hard to overcome the resentment he felt toward them. They had rejected the truth of Jesus, and he doubted it would do any good to go home to see them. Here was an opportunity to serve God. He felt he must go forward and not look back.

Dee also volunteered to go on the mission trip, for he didn't want to go home alone. It wasn't difficult to be a Christian when he was with Peng and others who believed in Jesus. Only fifteen years old, Dee was still very shy and quiet, but he cheerfully gave his testimony when asked.

Than Armand obtained travel passes for five students and two missionaries who were going in the mission van. They spent a night at a Christian village along the way, for travel was slow on the rough roads, and there were also many army roadblocks due to the war. Sometimes they had to wait nearly an hour at a checkpoint while the soldiers examined their passes. Frequently the soldiers were only young boys who could barely read, but they carried guns and had hand grenades clipped to their belts. No one questioned their authority.

The missionaries took the students to Ban Don, a country town much smaller than Savannakhet. Peng thought it was pleasant to be away from the noise and bustle of the city. Here there was only an occasional oxcart, jeep or bus. They held meetings to encourage the small group of believers in the town, and frequently they trekked to hill tribes in the countryside. Sometimes the river was the most direct route to a distant village, and Peng and the others enjoyed gliding along in a dugout canoe on shimmering water that reflected the tall trees and thick jungle vines leaning overhead. The war seemed far away.

The tribal people around Ban Don liked to listen to Peng teach the Bible. He was quick to understand their language and was soon using phrases from their speech when he answered questions. He made the Scriptures seem clearer than when the missionaries and other students taught in Laotian. After they had been in Ban Don a month, *Than* Armand told Peng that the church in Savannakhet had offered to support him as an evangelist if he wanted to stay there to preach.[2] Peng liked preaching better than studying, so he quickly decided he would not return to Bible School but settle in the Ban Don area where many villages had not yet heard the name of Jesus.

Soon after that he was surprised to receive a letter from *Than* John.

"I want to visit your parents in Ban Dao," John wrote. "Perhaps now they will receive the Gospel. Could you come to Kong and go with me?"

All that day Peng struggled wtih the decision. He was enjoying the work in Ban Don, and there were only problems at home. It would be wonderful if his parents would become Christians, but what if they again rejected the truth? He wrestled with God for hours in the night before he finally yielded.

When he announced his decision the next day, *Than* Armand approved, and Dee, always ready to follow, decided to return home with him. They left on a bus for Solane the next

---

[2] This was an unusual offer, for all Laotian pastors were unsalaried laymen.

morning, but it took three days of travel to reach Kong.

Later that week they began hiking across the mountain with John Davis and a new missionary, David Fewster. Even at this high elevation it was hot and humid. They plunged through thick forests, then came to open meadows where tall grasses waved gently in the hot breeze. At times the grass grew higher than their heads, and they could see only the rutted path ahead of them. The trees became sparse and the few scraggly bushes they passed gave little shade. The blue sky arched above them like a canopy of fire, and they were grateful when large white clouds formed in the afternoon and drifted across the heavens, blocking the glare of the burning sun.

They stopped several times to rest and preach along the way, spending one night in a village before reaching the edge of the mountains. As they began the descent over the eastern rim, a sudden rainshower drenched them. They huddled together under a large tree, glad that their Bibles and hymnbooks were in John's waterproof backpack.

The rain stopped as suddenly as it had started, and the sun came out. Sparkling drops of water glistened on every leaf. The air smelled fresh and clean, but the narrow path ahead was a river of mud. Slipping and sliding, they made their way slowly down the steep trail, and soon everyone was covered with mud. Peng laughed as John tripped over a tree root and fell on his face. The foreigner looked so funny with mud on his face!

But then Peng himself lost his balance and sat down in a big puddle! Everyone laughed together.

David noticed that little Dee was falling more than anyone. His thin arms and legs were trembling, and he wasn't smiling at all. David moved closer and began to help Dee keep his balance on the difficult trail.

Peng finally glimpsed his home village through the trees below them as they neared the end of the steep path. He wondered if anyone would recognize him covered with mud! But, more important, would his parents accept the truth of God when they heard it this time?

18

Victory in Ban Dao

DRIPPING WITH MUD, the men encountered laughter and teasing as they entered Ban Dao late that afternoon. Several children recognized Peng and ran to tell his parents he had come home. But he led his friends to the river first so everyone could take a bath.

Suk and Samat were living in the new house built at the edge of the fields. They received Peng joyfully and invited the missionaries to stay for the night. Tired from their long hike, they didn't protest when Suk insisted that they sleep on her new mattresses. They lay down gratefully soon after eating supper and slept soundly through the night, even though their long legs stretched out over the edge of the thin mattresses.

The next morning Peng's parents listened politely as John told of God's love in sending His Son Jesus to the earth. "Jesus took your sins upon Himself when He died, and God accepted His shed blood as payment for your sins. After three days in the grave Jesus came back to life and now He has power to deliver you from bondage to the devil and his evil spirits. Don't you want to be free?"

There was a long silence as Samat stared at the floor. Then his eyes met John's. "The Jesus way is good. I'm willing for my family to follow Jesus, but I must continue in the Taway traditions."

John turned to Peng's mother. "How about you, Suk?"

She licked her lips nervously and glanced at her husband. "I would like to follow the Jesus way," she said softly.

Peng's sister Ying stirred restlessly in the corner where she had been listening. "I want to become a Christian, too," she said.

Samat looked startled at this response, but he said nothing. Tears of joy filled Peng's eyes as his mother and sister prayed asking Jesus to cleanse them from sin and save them. God was answering his prayers. Surely his father would also believe soon!

John and David visited friends in Mong for a few days and then flew out on a plane and returned to Kong, leaving Peng and Dee in Ban Dao.

The harvesting began a week later, and Peng worked hard in the fields for his father, eager to express his love for him in a practical way. He also made a trip up the mountain for pine logs as the family was running out of chips to use for light.

He discovered his sister Ying had been married while he was away at Bible School. Jen, the young man she had named as the father of her child, had refused at first to marry her, unwilling to pay the dowry price or perhaps not feeling ready to support a family. Samat and the village elders had had long talks with him on several occasions, reminding him that according to Taway custom, he would have to pay a large fee if he didn't marry Ying. Since he had to pay some money in either case, he finally decided it was just as well to take her for his wife. Only a part of the dowry was required before the marriage; if there was a separation later or a breach of contract he would have to pay the balance.

Jen wasn't happy about Ying's decision to follow the Jesus way, but soon he became curious about this new religion and began coming to meetings with her.

The women usually gathered firewood by themselves, but several times Peng went with his mother to carry the wood home. He had been teaching her from the Bible, and she asked many questions as they walked along the forest path.

Great excitement ran through the village one day when someone noticed that the rock flowers had begun to bloom on the boulders near their houses. The spirit priests held special séances to try and contact the Great Spirit, but in vain. Peng told them repeatedly that Jesus was the Promised One who would bring deliverance, but they refused to believe this. Samat was halfway convinced, but he still hesitated to break with the old ways.

After the rice had been harvested Peng began to visit Ron and Kathy in Mong more frequently again. One day when he mentioned a Jalat village located a short distance north of the old capital, Ron realized he had never preached there and asked Peng to go with him. The Jalat were distantly related to the Taway tribe, and their languages were similar. It happened that Peng had gone there with his father many years before.

Expecting to be back in a few hours, the men took only a few bananas and a canteen of water with them. Kathy stayed home with the baby. They crossed the Say River in a small motorboat and then rode a truck to Kalao, the former capital of the province. Since Ron had preached there before, they hurried through the town and were soon on a path that led across the dry fields.

Waves of heat rose from the brown, dry countryside around them. A thin layer of dust covered the trees and bushes. The dry season made travel easier, but Peng looked forward to the coming of the monsoon rains when the paddies would become emerald green with new rice springing out of the shimmering water.

The trail seemed endless. Several hours later they still had not found the village, and Peng realized he didn't know where it was. As the sun was setting they found an empty hut in a field and decided to spend the night there.

"We'd better not build a fire," Peng warned. "I've heard that the 'forest people' are sometimes in this area." Like many people in Laos, he often used a neutral term to describe the communist soldiers. One never knew who might be listening.

"We don't have anything to cook, anyway," Ron said with a laugh. They had already eaten their bananas. Both of them longed for a drink of water, but they tried not to think about it, for the canteen Ron had brought along was now empty. Peng was used to traveling without water but this time he was glad Ron had insisted on bringing the canteen. Perhaps tomorrow they would be able to refill it with river water. He felt embarrassed that he had been such a poor guide. When he had come here with his father he had been very young, and the trail hadn't seemed so long.

They committed themselves into the Lord's care and then tried to get some rest. The rough bamboo floor of the hut was uneven, and it took them a long time to fall asleep.

Ron awoke with a start and sniffed the air. Someone was smoking a cigarette under the hut! Were there soldiers outside?

Peng whispered, "Don't move! If they hear a noise they'll know we are here." They were both quite frightened. No one but the 'forest people' would be out in the fields at night. If they were discovered, they might be captured or even killed. Peng prayed silently for God's protection and knew Ron was doing the same.

Finally the smell of cigarette smoke faded. There was no sound below the hut. Had the men left? They didn't dare move but lay still, their muscles stiffening. Neither of them got any sleep the rest of the night.

Early the next morning they set out again, changing their direction, and soon crossed a shallow stream. The water obviously had mosquito larvae in it, but Ron filled the canteen anyway and dropped in a tablet to purify the water. A half-hour later they stopped in the shade of a tree and gulped the water down. Even though they knew the tablet couldn't kill the larvae, the water tasted good.

When they finally reached the Jalat village, they were given a royal reception. Amazed and grateful that a foreigner would come so far to see them, many people gathered in the headman's large house to listen to the Gospel records in their language. Ron and Peng spent the entire day sharing the good news of Jesus with the villagers. The people were very hospitable, bringing them rice and stewed chicken to eat and urging them to stay overnight, so Ron decided to spend a night there, thinking that some of them might turn to the true God.

After dark the crowd returned to the headman's house to hear more. Peng was explaining the way of salvation again to the people when suddenly loud wailing from a nearby house pierced the air. Looking at one another fearfully, everyone quickly scrambled down the ladder and disappeared, leaving Peng and Ron with their host.

"My brother's son has been sick for several days, and I believe he has just died," the headman explained. "I must go now, but you may sleep here tonight."

Ron looked at Peng in distress as he left. "If only they had told us about the sick boy earlier, we could have prayed for him," he said. "What will we do if they declare the village *kalaam* and say we can't leave tomorrow?"

"I don't know," Peng answered, "but we can't leave right now in the dark."

Praying for guidance, they sat alone all evening as the wailing continued. A woman brought them more rice and stewed chicken to eat, but wouldn't stay to listen to the records. They longed to go comfort the bereaved family, but the headman had warned them to stay away.

"We'd better pray that we won't be accused of causing the child's death," Peng said. "Satan is doing his best to keep us from telling these people about Jesus." Before they went to sleep that night they spent a long time in prayer for the grieving villagers, that they might soon be delivered from Satan's power.

The next morning they were startled when six people brought them chickens and rice to eat. They ate what they could and tried politely to decline the rest, but their host insisted they accept it all.

"You have a long walk before you reach home tonight. You will need food along the way." The headman's wife wrapped some cold rice in banana leaves and gave them the pieces of roasted chicken tied into a handy bundle with vine. Although chickens in Laos were rather small and scrawny, Ron knew it was a sacrifice for the villagers to give them so much, but there was no polite way to refuse the food without offending them.

Without further adventures they reached Mong late that afternoon, much to Kathy's relief, for she had been quite anxious about their safety. Although they had planned to be away only one afternoon, they had been gone for two nights.

Peng enjoyed these evangelistic trips and was often away from Ban Dao several days at a time. When he returned home one morning in May, Ron went with him. As they approached the new house built at the edge of the fields they saw Suk sitting on the porch, looking glum. She said nothing until they had climbed the ladder.

"Your father almost died last night," she told Peng then, obviously frightened and worried.

They found Samat lying on a mattress in a corner of the house, feverish, and sleeping restlessly. Ron and Peng were praying quietly for him when he finally awoke. He smiled weakly, relieved to see his son was home again.

"The evil spirits are angry because I've broken several taboos," he said. "If I die today I know I'll go to hell, and then I'll never escape from their power. I want to follow Jesus. He is the Great Spirit who promised to come when the rock flowers bloomed."

Peng gripped his father's hand and smiled, tears running down his brown cheeks. His heart was so full he couldn't speak.

"Go get my charms from the mountain house and burn them," Samat said. "I'm too weak to do it myself. Be sure to get the ones out of the granary, too, and also the magic stones buried in the rice field."

The charms and other objects Samat had used in his work as a spirit priest were kept in a dirty cloth shoulder bag Peng found hanging from the rafters of their village house. Ron followed him to the granary and then watched him dig up the magic stones that were buried in a clay pot in the field. Peng knew right where the pot was buried, near a paddy dike.

He sorted out the things that would burn, and they tossed them into a fire they built at the edge of the forest. The stones and other objects that wouldn't burn they threw into a thicket in the woods where no one would find them.

Peng kept the shoulder bag as a reminder of their deliverance from the old life, since it had belonged to his great-grandfather and had no magical use. Suk had asked them also to save the beauty paste, a homemade rouge which she used for festive occasions.

"It has nothing to do with spirit worship and probably it won't offend Jesus," she said.

As the charms burned Peng read some Bible verses aloud and spoke to the spirits. "Go away from us and never return! Samat is now trusting in Jesus, the true God. You no longer have any power over him, because Jesus' blood is protecting him."

From then on Samat began to get well. His brother Vahn was pleased to hear the good news when Peng visited him in the garden the next day.

"I'm going to follow Jesus too," Vahn decided. "I want to be free from the evil spirits." He had observed the change in Peng's life and wanted to experience it himself.

A few weeks later Vahn's sister and her husband also trusted Christ.

Samat's older brother Loong watched the new believers closely. He was the one who had first challenged Peng to follow the true God. A year ago he had been frightened when his cousin Nuen died after leaving the Jesus way to return to the spirits. But now he was impressed by the change in his brothers' lives. Both Vahn and Samat appeared happy and very confident, and peace shone in their eyes instead of fear.

Loong and his wife finally decided it was safe to follow the Jesus way. Along with their five children they prayed, receiving Jesus as their Savior and Lord, and promptly burned their ancestor shelf and everything related to spirit worship.

When the village elders saw so many of the Taway becoming Christians, they were alarmed and began to circulate threats against the believers, hoping to discourage them. Heng was one of the leaders of the opposition.

"Let's drive them out of the village," he said.

But still more turned to Christ. One afternoon twin babies were born to a young mother. Taway custom decreed that one of the babies should die as an offering to the spirits, as such births were unnatural. The father came to Samat that night for advice.

"Can we let both our babies live if we enter the Jesus way?" he asked.

"Yes, but you must turn away from the evil spirits and truly repent of your sins," Samat told him. "Jesus cannot help you unless you trust in Him with all your heart."

Peng and Samat counseled with the man and his wife, and finally they burned their spirit shelf and fetishes, committing themselves and their babies to the Lord.

Peng didn't return to Bible School in the spring, for he felt it was more important to stay home to teach the new Christians. Samat was tired in the evenings after working in the fields all day, but he often asked Peng to read the Bible to him, and with his help and encouragement he soon taught himself to read.

The former spirit priest was especially interested in verses that spoke of man's inner spirit. He had always thought that humans had only a body and soul, and that sickness and problems came in life because it was difficult for men to relate to the spirit beings around them. He was fascinated by the discovery that he had a spirit as well as a soul in his body, and he became quite excited when he realized that men's problems were simply the result of their spirits being dead in sin and out of communication with God the Creator. After much reflection on the matter, he decided to present his views at the next "singing debate" in Ban Dao. These round-table discussions were held in the evenings at seasons when there was time to relax and socialize. Samat was an expert in debate and had always been a favorite of the villagers.

Peng went with him. They found the headman's large wooden house crowded with men smoking their clay pipes, a few teenagers and women sitting near the doorway. As Peng and his father entered, some of the men muttered a greeting, but others stared at Samat briefly and then turned away, refusing to acknowledge the presence of this one who had opposed their traditions.

While Peng squatted near the back, Samat took his place confidently with the other singers in the center of the musty, smoke-filled room. The only light came from a *kabong* torch propped up on a small hand-carved wooden stand. *Kabongs* were made from pine chips, sticklak, and tree resin molded into a long narrow torch wrapped with large leaves and tied firmly with flexible strips of bamboo or vine. These torches burned slowly and were often used at meetings and festive occasions. They gave a brighter light than pine chips and needed little attention except an occasional tap to knock the ash off the burning end.

When Samat's turn came, he chanted with a wavering melody,

> "Our body was formed of earth's dark dust
> By the hand of the Creator-God.
> He breathed into us a reasoning soul,
> That life might move our bones.
> God also gave us each a spirit
> So that He could talk with us.
> But the king of darkness tempted man
> To follow the spirits of evil,
> And so the spirit within us died
> When we chose the way of sin.

Fear and trouble will always be with us
While our spirit is bound by darkness.
Jesus alone can overcome death
And give our spirit life."

Batik, the spirit priest from the upper end of the village, glared at Samat. A flicker of interest rose at the back of his mind, but he would not let it show in his eyes. What if this new doctrine were true? He squelched the thought immediately. He would lose his authority in the village if he admitted their traditions were wrong, or if he showed any interest in this new teaching. Thinking quickly, he composed his rebuttal and sang it firmly.

"There are thirty-two parts of our body,
And each one has a soul.
When we are asleep our souls like to wander
If they do not return, our body will die.
At death our souls are claimed
By the mysterious spirits of darkness.
Joined to them, we have power over men
Power to help and power to hurt.
The spirits of the trees, the rocks and the
    mountains
Demand our reverence and our respect.
Give yourself to the spirits of darkness
And others will fear and serve you well."

After several others had chanted their agreement with Batik, Samat sang a bold response, trying to present God's truth on a level easily understood.

"My spirit lay in darkness, dead.
It could not find the light.
Then Jesus put His life within.
And now I talk with God.
He makes my spirit understand
The mysteries of life.
Our Creator loves us all, my friends,
He can rescue us from death.
Oh, turn away from darkness now
And confess your sins to God.
In Jesus you'll find peace and joy,
He'll set you free from fear."

Time after time the other singers contradicted Samat, trying to prove him wrong. Truths newly learned from God's Word flooded his mind as he attempted to explain some of the puzzles of life that had always troubled his tribe. No one could find a hole in his reasoning, but this only angered the other men. They didn't want to admit their error or change their ancient system of belief.

Never had there been such a heated debate in the village of Ban Dao! When the meeting closed late that night, several men secretly resolved that if Samat would not return to the old ways they would someday kill him. His ideas were too dangerous. Soon the whole village would want to follow this one named Jesus.

Peng spent another semester at Bible School that fall, when in spite of still being a slow student he was chosen as student body president. He returned home in time to help with the harvest, and found the Taway Christians had remained strong in spite of numerous trials. One problem was the shortage of water. The dry season had started earlier than usual. By the middle of December the ponds were already dry, and the river was extremely low. Only a trickle of water came down from the spring up on the side of the mountain, not nearly enough for the village. The women had to walk twelve kilometers to the river to fill their buckets and gourds with drinking water, an all-day trip which left them no time or energy for household chores or helping with the harvest. The men were hot and thirsty after working in the fields each day and they longed to take a cool bath, but there wasn't sufficient water for drinking, let along bathing. The unbelievers grumbled and blamed the Christians for their troubles.

In spite of these hardships, Christmas was a happy time for Peng that year. At last there was a church in his village! On Christmas afternoon Ron and Kathy came to hold a special service at the garden house so Vahn could attend. His little house couldn't hold all the believers, so they met outside on the ground even though it was a cold, windy day.

After telling the Christmas story, Ron felt the new Christians needed additional encouragement, so he read from the fourth chapter of Philippians and asked Peng to translate his words into Taway. "Brethren dearly beloved, my joy and crown, stand fast in the Lord."

As Ron went on to speak of the women who had labored in the Gospel with Paul, Suk smiled. She had been witnessing to her neighbors and liked to feel she was doing something important for Jesus.

"Always rejoice in the Lord," Ron continued. He reminded them, "Whatever trials may come to you, God has a purpose for them, and He is in control."

"Don't be anxious about anything but pray about everything with thanksgiving," Peng translated. "God's peace will keep your hearts and minds through Christ Jesus. God will supply all our needs according to His riches in glory."

"God will even provide the water you need," Ron added.

Peng knew how important it was to teach God's Word to his people. Only by feeding on the words of God would they find strength to stand firm through whatever troubles might lie ahead.

19

Suffering For Christ

SAMAT REALIZED HE had to find water somehow. Everyone was hot and thirsty from long hours of cutting rice in the fields, and there was never enough drinking water. No one had time to carry it from the river every day.

He discussed the matter with the other believers, and they decided to ask God to help them dig a well. According to Taway tradition it was *kalaam* to dig a hole where one had not previously existed, but the Christians realized this was just a pagan superstition. They met for a prayer meeting very early the next morning and then went outside to survey their land. The earth everywhere was dry and cracked; even the fish holes had already dried up. Very few fish had been harvested that year. Samat finally suggested they dig in the corner of one of his rice fields. A well there would be near his field house and convenient for the others also. Everyone helped dig the hole, even Loong's children.

The other villagers watched in horror, shocked that the Christians would dare to break the tribal taboo. Although the Taway were allowed to clean out the deep holes that existed in some fields to trap fish, the evil spirits would surely be offended if new holes were dug in the ground. USAID had once brought a drilling rig out to a Taway village to dig a well for them, but the people had stoned them and forced them to leave.

"You're making the spirits angry. You'll never find water there," the unbelievers said fearfully as they watched the Christians from a safe distance.

But Samat and the others continued to dig all day under the hot sun, abandoning their other chores. The women and children worked as hard as the men, loosening the soil with their hoes and throwing the dirt over the edge with buckets and their bare hands. Everyone sang and prayed as they labored, believing God would supply their need.

The well was nearly shoulder-deep when finally water began to collect at the bottom. Suk hurried over to her house. Her neighbors laughed and jeered as she grabbed two buckets, carried them down the ladder from the porch on a shoulder pole, and set off back across the fields.

"She's going to bring back dirt to drink!" they shouted in derision.

Suk found the hole filling with water as the believers laughed and cried with joy. Everyone quickly filled their gourds and buckets, but still more water rose in the well bottom. When Suk's neighbors saw her return home with water, they stopped their mocking. Water! They couldn't believe their eyes. The word spread quickly, and a stampede began. A crowd of people converged on Samat's field, and without asking for water they pushed the believers aside and helped themselves.

Shocked at such bad manners, the Christians stood back and watched. They were quite willing to share the water; they only hoped their generosity would help win their neighbors to Jesus.

Unexpectedly, *Than* John arrived for a brief visit just then. Hearing the commotion and seeing a line of people with buckets surrounding the new well, he went over to inspect it. Obviously it had been dug in just the right place, for the level of the clear, fresh water was less than two meters from the surface of the dry, parched rice field.

The next morning, as John was talking with Peng in the house, Samat came in for his morning meal, having turned his buffaloes out to graze. Without speaking to anyone he sat down in a corner and opened up his big Lao Bible. He read quietly for a long time, until finally Suk reminded him it was time to go work in the fields again, and he had better eat his rice.

"Oh, I'm full from reading the Scriptures. I don't want any rice," Samat said, laying his Bible down and hurrying out through the low doorway.

John was astonished that in spite of his age and background Samat had already learned to read Laotian and was obviously so hungry for communion with God that he could become totally engrossed in the Scriptures.

"When did your father learn to read?" he asked Peng.

"A few months ago, after he became a believer," Peng answered proudly. "He really taught himself, although I helped him a bit. He loves to read

God's Word. He says it's just as if God is talking to him."

Later in the morning, after John had left, the village elders came to claim the well. "It's right on the edge of the field and is really part of the forest land which belongs to the village," they said. "All of us have the right to use the water."

Samat protested that the well was clearly on his own private land, but said he was willing to share with everyone. Soon it became apparent that there wasn't enough water in the well for so many people. The believers again had to make occasional trips to the river, for all day long the well was surrounded by villagers waiting for the water level to rise enough for them to be able to fill their buckets. As he harvested rice in a field nearby, Peng could hear people shouting and bickering over whose turn it was to draw from the well. Instead of showing some gratitude, the unbelievers continued to mock Samat and his family.

"Why don't you dig us another well?" they called out as they watched him thresh his rice. "Then we would have plenty of water!"

"This water doesn't belong to Jesus," another villager said. "See, He doesn't stop it from flowing even though I'm not His follower. I can take all I want."

"If you like to dig wells, why don't you come dig one in my rice field? I'll let you dig all you want!"

It was hard to take this abuse meekly. Samat's temper flared more than once, and even Peng's gentle spirit became hot, but whenever he let out a sharp retort he was immediately ashamed. He knew Jesus loved these people in spite of their ingratitude and unbelief, so he tried to be patient and kind.

The Christians complained to him about the continued shortage of water. He encouraged them the best he could with Scripture, reading from Genesis how Jacob had had many of his wells taken from him.

"God will take care of us," he said, although he himself often felt discouraged. No one had time to dig another well.

At last the harvesting was finished and the rice was safely stored in the granaries. In February Peng took his father to the church conference in Savannakhet. He was hungry for Christian fellowship and he also wanted Samat to see that they weren't alone in following Jesus, but that there were many other believers. He was especially eager for him to meet the leaders of the churches.

They didn't know what to make of Samat at first. Tribal people were often considered somewhat inferior by some Laotians. Although the church elders knew better and were just country people themselves, they were tempted to look with disdain on this tall stranger with the bushy hair and broken teeth stained black with betel-nut.

However, Samat's radiant smile and eager friendliness soon won everyone over. His vocabulary in Laotian was limited, but Peng was always at hand to interpret for him. The Christians were deeply stirred when Samat gave his testimony at one of the meetings. Few of them had ever heard of a spirit priest being converted to Christ! His knowledge of the Scriptures also amazed them. Everyone soon had a deep respect for this father and son whose lives had been changed so completely by Christ.

After the conference Peng returned home with Samat, hiking over the mountains. He didn't return to Bible School until the fall semester again that year, feeling that his father and the other believers still needed him.

Ron and Kathy Smith were now living in Ban Tay, a short distance south of Mong. In this village they felt closer to the people. The house they had rented near the river was a typical Laotian home, built up on stilts with a wide verandah in front. As in most Laotian houses, there were numerous cracks between the planks which formed the walls and floors, but these let in light and air which were appreciated during the humid summer months. Occasionally they were uncomfortable during the cool dry season, but it was never very cold in this part of Laos.

The shady space under the house was ideal for holding meetings; it was also a convenient and safe play area for their son Steve as he grew up. Even when he was only two years old, Laotian children would come to play with him as Kathy sat nearby chatting with their mothers.

Whenever Peng was home from Bible School he would come to study the Bible with Ron and Kathy on Sundays, bringing some of the new believers with him. Often they stayed overnight, for there was room for everyone to sleep in the missionaries' large living room.

That year more Gospel recordings were made in the Taway language so the Christians would have new teaching and evangelistic tools. They still didn't have any Scriptures written in their language, as it had not yet been reduced to writing, although Ron and Kathy were attempting to study and analyze it.

In Ban Dao Samat continued to witness boldly for Christ, and as a result his older daughter Noy finally decided to enter the Jesus way. However, her unbelieving husband held her back, and she rarely came to any meetings. Ying's husband Jen also became a Christian at this time, as well as Pak, Ling and another teenage boy. Dee and Sahn, however, had given in to the pressure of the village elders and never came to the meetings.

Samat's older brother Loong was very enthusiastic about his new faith. He had a forceful, outgoing personality, and often went out evangelizing with Ron when Peng was away at Bible School. Once they were riding Ron's small Honda motorbike through the forest and saw a log lying across the path. Ron thought they could jump it, but the log bounced up in front of them and they crashed. Both of them tore their pants and scraped their knees badly. They were sore and limping for nearly a month, but Loong just laughed about it and continued to go out with Ron whenever he could get away from his work in the fields.

Sometimes Ron and Kathy went up the river by boat to visit Uncle Vahn and hold a Sunday service at his house. Although crippled in his feet and unable to travel far, he had been witnessing to his neighbors in the potters' village nearby and occasionally some of them would come to the meetings.

By the time Peng graduated from Bible School there were about twenty Taway people believing in Jesus, and several others showing interest in the Gospel. The village leaders were alarmed when they saw so many joining the band of Christians. They tried to frighten Peng with threats against his life, believing that without a leader the people would return to the tribal ways. Peng heard a rumor that someone was going to kill him, but he refused to be intimidated. He continued to work in his fields and teach the believers in his spare time, confident that God would protect them all.

One night, while sleeping in the field house, he was awakened several hours before dawn by something striking his foot. Sitting up in surprise, he saw rocks falling through the thatch roof.

"Quick! Get under your mattress!" he heard his father call out from behind the sleeping partition at the back of the house. More rocks were falling on him, so Peng hurriedly rolled off his mattress and pulled it over on top of himself. It wasn't very thick and was barely wide enough to cover his body, but he was grateful for its protection.

He heard people yelling curses outside as large stones continued to drop through the grass roof.

Finally the bombardment ceased, but he lay there for a long time, not sure whether the attack would be resumed.

The next morning he learned that the other Christian families had also been stoned. Fortunately no one had been seriously hurt, but everyone was frightened. Peng and Samat counted 153 fist-sized rocks that had been thrown into their house alone; the other families also collected many buckets of stones. If anyone had been hit on the head, he could have been gravely injured.

Afraid to stay in their homes another night, the shaken believers went to tell the missionaries what had happened. Peng took a couple of the rocks along to show Ron and Kathy.

"What shall we do?" he asked anxiously.

They went with him to report the attack to the police. The Laotian officials questioned the Christians carefully and then sent a representative out to talk to the village elders. Tuat, the headman, did not deny the stoning but he said he couldn't identify the ones who had done it.

"We've had much sickness in our village because of the Christians," he said. "They have offended the spirits and even caused one of them to disappear. The spirit Peng drove out of a granary four years ago has been untraceable ever since. It's the believers' fault, and we don't want them to live among us any longer."

The Laotian officials, being Buddhists, believed that tolerance was an important virtue. "We have freedom of religion for everyone in our country," they argued. "You cannot force these people off their own land." After much angry discussion Tuat finally yielded a bit.

"I guess they can remove into the forest half a kilometer on the other side of their rice fields and start a new village there," he said grudgingly.

For several weeks the Christians labored at clearing the forest and cutting timber for their new houses. Even when it rained they rarely stopped to rest, and somehow they also managed to get their rice crop planted. Vahn decided to move up from the garden to live near the others, and he built himself a new house with very little help in spite of his crippled legs.

In the meantime they were still living in their old field huts, although the children were frightened at night and their parents were anxious. No more stones had been thrown, but everyone was relieved when at last the new village was completed. Early the next morning they carried their mattresses, pots and other belongings out to their new homes. In the afternoon Ron and Kathy Smith came to hold a dedication service and commit the new village into God's care. As the Taway believers sang Christian hymns and listened to the Scriptures, they found new courage and resolved to be faithful to Jesus, whatever the cost.

That evening Peng went to visit a relative in another village. Since the threats on his life had increased, he had started sleeping in a different place every night, hoping it might draw attention away from the other Christians if he were not always with them.

When he returned home early the next morning he found his mother crouched on the porch of their new house, sobbing and wailing. The other Christians stood in quiet groups nearby, looking terrified.

"What is wrong?" he cried in alarm.

"Come and see," Loong said sorrowfully, leading him down to the stream a few yards from the house.

There Peng saw his father's body, mangled and bloody, lying in the water. He had been shot four times and his skull had been crushed. Loong told Peng that four men had come during the night, pulled Samat out of his house, beaten him and shot him, threatening to do the same to all the Christians if they didn't turn back to the evil spirits.

If only I had been home, perhaps they would just have killed me and left my father alive, Peng agonized. But he knew the unbelievers had wanted to kill his father as well as himself. Samat's total rejection of the witchcraft he had practiced all his life was a threat to the elders' power over the Taway people, and they considered him particularly responsible for the epidemic of dysentery which had recently swept through the village.

Peng was too stunned to cry. Loong helped him carry the body up into the house and wash it for burial. Then, afraid to stay in their new homes, the Christians walked into town to ask the missionaries for help.

Ron and Kathy were eating breakfast on their verandah when they saw the Taway believers approaching. "Something has happened," Ron told Kathy as he climbed down the ladder to greet them.

"They killed my father," Peng said. His eyes filled with tears, but his face was hard with anger. He still couldn't believe his father was dead.

Ron sent a telegram to Pakse immediately to notify the other missionaries and Peng's brother. Then he took the Christians to report the murder to the town officials, who wrote it up in their books. Suk testified that three of the murderers had been strangers, hit men apparently hired by the unbelievers, but she thought the fourth man was Heng. Loong agreed.

Ron went back with Peng that afternoon. They wrapped the body in two old woollen blankets and put it in a wooden box, then with a simple service of prayer and Scripture reading, they buried Samat's body in the forest upstream from the new village, near the tribal burial grounds. Peng was still in a daze. The only thing that enabled him to go on was the knowledge that he would be reunited with his father someday in heaven in the presence of Jesus, where there would be no more sin or suffering.

Khap arrived the next day with OMF missionaries Robin East and David Fewster and several Laotian elders. Together they went out to the burial site and held a memorial service to honor the memory of the converted spirit priest who had given his all for Christ. The elder of the church in Savannakhet counseled the Christians and encouraged them to stand firm. Their spirits revived somewhat after this, but they were still in a state of shock, afraid to return to their homes.

Although the police had sent someone to investigate the matter, no further action was taken, and Peng and Khap finally decided to leave it with the Lord and not press any charges. They were sure that eventually justice would be done.

The village elders declared that north Ban Dao, the main village at the foot of the mountains, was *kalaam*, forbidden to the Christians for one year, and any of them who entered it would be killed. None of the Taway villages were willing to take the Christians in, so this meant that they would have to live in the forest all by themselves, completely isolated from their friends and relatives. This was a frightening new idea, for in Taway culture people were interdependent and no one did anything alone.

The Laotian officials, tired of trying to settle the conflict between the two factions of the Taway tribe, recommended that the believers move to another area, but they offered no concrete help in finding such a place. So, although uneasy about returning to the new village where Samat had been murdered, the Christians decided they had no choice. There was no other place to go. Their rice fields needed tending, and they couldn't stay with the missionaries indefinitely. Anyway, they didn't want to flee just because they had met opposition. Surely if they stood firm, many more of the Taway people would begin to trust in Jesus?

Somewhat fearfully, they went back to the little clearing in the forest. Following Jesus was costing them a great deal, but they were determined to follow Samat's example of courage, that his death might not be in vain.

One morning after a night of heavy rain and violent winds, Peng was going through his fields repairing the dikes. With his hoe he piled mud up at the sides of a dike which had been weakened by water flooding down from the higher fields. As he started to walk on, raising the hoe to his shoulder, he heard a loud *ping* and felt something hard hit the metal end of the hoe.

Glancing down, he saw a bullet at his feet. With a gasp of astonishment he looked about him but could see no one. Realizing his attacker must be hiding far off in the forest at the edge of the fields, he put the bullet in his pocket and hurried home, silently praising God for saving his life.

When the other believers heard what had happened, they were very frightened. The next day they all went into town to tell Ron about the shooting and ask his advice. Handing the bullet to him, Peng asked him to keep it.

"You should report this to the police," Ron said.

"It won't do any good. They haven't arrested anyone for my father's murder yet, even though they know who did it. Anyway, maybe the person who shot at me will turn to Jesus now that he sees God can protect me."

"But this could have killed you! Where would the bullet have hit if the hoe hadn't been in the way?"

Peng pointed to his heart. But his square jaw was firmly set with determination. "The person who shot the rifle must have been a long way off, because the bullet was nearly spent when it reached me. God will protect me."

But the Christians agreed that they had to find another place to live. They stayed with Ron and Kathy for several days before gaining courage to return to their homes. Fearing for their lives, they begged Peng to find a safer place for them to settle.

A few days later Peng and his mother flew to Solane to look for a village that would take them in. He had heard there were numerous refugee villages along the winding mountain roads on the western side of the mountains. In Ban Khat, a few kilometers from Solane, a group of Christian Huay refugees listened to Peng's story with astonishment and sympathy. They said they would gladly welcome the Taway believers to live with them, and would help them build homes and make fields to plant their rice.

When Peng returned with this news, most of the believers decided to accept the invitation. However, the family with twins decided not to go, even though it would mean renouncing their faith. Peng realized they might have turned to Jesus just so their babies wouldn't be killed. There was apparently little danger to the twins now.

Sahn had never been a strong Christian, and he had left to join the army many months ago. Lam was still not a believer; he seemed more afraid than before to trust in Jesus. Peng hadn't seen Dee for a long time, for he was still going along with witchcraft and living with his unsaved uncle and aunt.

Although Peng's oldest sister Noy claimed she still believed in Jesus, she decided to stay in Ban Dao until she could persuade her husband to come out with her. The three teenage boys decided to stay also. Peng didn't blame them for wanting to remain near their relatives, but he knew they would be expected to make offerings to appease the spirits. Perhaps I failed them somehow, he told himself, his heart aching.

Hoping that Bek and Lang would yield at last to Christ, he visited them, but they continued to harden their hearts. Peng even scraped up enough courage to witness to Heng, although Suk reminded him that she had seen Heng with the men who had murdered Samat.

Heng didn't invite him into his house but stood outside to talk, his face ashen and his expression grim. When Peng didn't accuse him or berate him for his part in Samat's murder, a look of astonishment and wonder crept over his face. His tight-lipped expression softened somewhat, but he answered gruffly, "I don't want anything to do with Jesus. He can't help you now. You are wasting your time talking to me."

"Jesus loves you," Peng responded, "but if you reject Him, He will have to judge you and punish your sin."

"I'm not afraid of your Jesus!" shouted Heng, feeling somewhat alarmed. Deep down he was shocked and ashamed of what he had done, but he masked such feelings of weakness with a fierce look. "Get out of my sight and don't bother me again." He put out his arm to push Peng away, but Peng quickly stepped backward, avoiding his touch.

As Heng turned and climbed the pole ladder to his house, Lansee came out on the porch to see if the men were going to fight. She had been listening from inside the house and was terrified that her husband would harm Peng. She didn't care much for Peng any longer, but she didn't want Heng to hurt him. Since the day she had heard rumors that her husband had somehow been involved in Samat's death, she didn't know what Heng might do, but she was well aware that he hated Peng and all the Christians and was capable of violence. She felt relieved when she saw Peng walk away slowly, his head bowed. But for some reason she felt sad too, as though an opportunity had slipped out of her grasp. What if Peng's message about Jesus was true? But of course it couldn't be true, she thought, dismissing her uneasiness and following her husband back into the darkened house.

It took a week or so for Ron to find transportation for the Christians who were leaving. Finally an official of USAID offered to evacuate the group in one of their planes.

Four families were leaving along with Peng and his mother: his younger sister Ying and her husband Jen; a widow with her two sons; Vahn with his sister and her husband, and Uncle Loong and his family. Counting everyone's children, there were nineteen Taway believers being evacuated. They took all the belongings they could carry, but each family was allowed only one sack of rice. No doubt the unbelievers in Ban Dao would help themselves to the rice left behind in their granaries, as well as what they had just planted.

As the plane lifted off from the airfield in Mong, Peng could see the mountains in the distance, bright green paddy fields strung along their base like an emerald necklace. Then the plane turned north along the edge of the mountains, and he glimpsed several Taway villages almost hidden among the thick growth of the rainforest.

It was hard to leave, for he had lived here all his life. Although generations in the distant past had lived high up on the mountains near the Huay people, even then the Taway had cultivated paddy fields on the plains below. They had never moved about making new fields every few years as the hill tribes did. Samat's fields had been passed down through many generations, but now they would belong to others. Someone else would harvest the rice he had so carefully planted.

Somehow Peng felt it wasn't right to leave. Why should they allow the unbelievers to force them away from their homes and fields? Shouldn't they stay and continue to witness for Jesus, as Ron and Kathy were doing?

But there seemed to be no place near Mong for them to settle. The Laotian officials and even the missionaries had encouraged them to leave.

Peng felt helpless to change the course of events. He wanted to stay, but his family and friends were determined to leave. For two months now since his father's brutal murder they had lived with the threat of death hanging over them. His mind was confused and his heart ached, but as he looked down at the jungle passing so swiftly below him he was sure that someday he would return to Ban Dao to win the rest of his tribe to the true God.

20

Fruitfulness

THE TAWAY CHRISTIANS were soon settled in Ban Khat, a short distance off the paved road which wound up the side of the mountain. The Huay believers welcomed them eagerly; they knew what it was like to be refugees, having themselves been forced by the war to leave the home of their forefathers. Already they were quite prosperous. They had planted durian trees several years ago, and now that the trees were mature, they were selling the fruit at a good profit in the Solane market, only ten kilometers away. When cut open, durian had a horrible smell, like rotten eggs or strong onions, but many Laotians and westerners had learned to like it. If a person held his nose while eating durian, the fruit was delicious!

The Huay Christians were gracious and generous, and their language was similar to Taway. However, Peng found it difficult to adapt to some of their customs, especially their way of growing rice, for they planted it on hillsides which had been cleared by the slash and burn method. He attempted to prepare a field for planting but found that after cutting down the timber he had to let it dry for three months. Several more months were required to clean up the field and burn the brush before he could begin to plant any rice. These jobs would have to be done each year as new fields were added. He saw that he would be so busy working in the fields the year round that he would have little time to evangelize the refugee villages in the area or return to Bible School.

He considered making a small paddy field down by the creek but knew he couldn't make a plow strong enough to break up the hard virgin ground. Even if his Uncle Vahn made him a sharp steel blade, a wooden plow would be sure to split when he hit buried rocks and tree stumps. It would be quite different from working in the paddy fields around Ban Dao which had been cultivated for many generations.

He shared his problem with *Than* John when he saw him in Solane one day. "I'd like to grow paddy field rice so I can take time off to go back to Bible School and preach in the villages. But I don't have a plow strong enough to break up the ground."

"Let me think about it for a while," John said. "Maybe there's something I can do to help."

The next time he went to Bangkok John looked for a small steel plow that could easily be pulled behind one buffalo. He bought one and gave it to Peng, who with its help was able to clear a piece of land down by the creek. Once the field was cleared, the dikes made and the water inlet and outlet engineered, he could wait until the rains came each year before he had to begin plowing and raking his fields for planting. This would give him time to attend Bible School and go out preaching in the dry season.

The Huay, who had to start working on their fields at the beginning of the dry season, soon observed the advantages of Peng's method, and several men asked him to teach them this type of agriculture which was entirely foreign to them. However, the small patches of level land on the side of the mountain were not well suited for paddy fields.

Loong bought a nice piece of land for his fields down near Solane where the land was quite flat. Vahn settled near him and later married the Christian widow who had come out from Ban Dao with her two sons. Although he still walked about on his knees using pieces of old tire tread for padding, Vahn managed to build himself a house and also opened a blacksmith shop which developed into a thriving business.

With the aid of a grant from a Lao church fund used to help needy Christians become self-sufficient, Peng was able to buy a rice field near Vahn's land, across the road to the west. It was a beautiful, fairly level piece of ground which included several paddies. Later another grant made it possible for him to buy a water buffalo so he wouldn't have to borrow or rent one. The young buffalo was untrained, not accustomed to pulling the plow through the muck and mud in the flooded paddy, but Peng worked hard and finally got his rice planted.

One day his water buffalo wandered off and

he couldn't find it. He looked everywhere but without success. The missionaries heard about it and everyone was praying that Peng would find his lost buffalo. Finally John told him it was hopeless to look any further, because it was quite likely the animal had been stolen and had already been cut up and sold for meat in the market at Solane.

"Oh no, *Than* John," Peng protested. "God knows where my buffalo is, and when the time is right He will show me just where to look for it."

"It's too late for that if people have already eaten it!" John scoffed. But he admired Peng's faith and hoped the animal would be found.

A few days later, as John and Dorothy were driving along a road in the country, they whizzed past a farmer wearing a pointed Vietnamese hat and leading a water buffalo. Several hundred feet down the road something clicked in John's mind. Recalling the smile on the farmer's face, he put his foot on the brake.

"I think we know that man," he said to Dorothy as he stopped the car and turned it around. When they finally drew up beside the plodding farmer and got a good look at the brown face under the big conical hat, they found that, sure enough, it was Peng! He had found his buffalo.

"God finally told me where to look," he said with a satisfied smile. He never would say any more about it.

Ron and Kathy Smith were now living in Solane. A few months after the Taway Christians had been evacuated, the military situation in the Mong area had deteriorated sharply and they had had to leave. Now once a week they rode their motorbike out to visit the Taway believers and encourage them, meeting one week in Vahn's house and the next week in Loong's.

Vahn's sister also lived nearby, and her husband Sohn often helped Vahn make charcoal for the blacksmith shop. Sohn began having trouble with the amulets that the spirit priests in Ban Dao had placed under his skin many years ago. About an inch long, these gold needles were supposed to wriggle around when danger was near, warning him to take precautions. But now the amulets had begun to irritate his skin.

Peng exhorted Sohn to turn away from faith in such things and wholly follow Jesus. Although Sohn had made a profession of faith, he was never a strong Christian, but finally he agreed to have some of the amulets removed. Ron took him to the clinic in Paksong where the Filipino doctors first x-rayed him to locate the needles and then removed most of them. Sohn's health improved after that, but his faith remained weak.

Ron began to make regular visits to several refugee villages along the winding mountain roads, taking Peng with him whenever possible. Large groups from several tribes had come out of the distant mountains along the Vietnamese border where fighting had recently intensified, and many new villages were springing up in the hills near Solane. Peng found he could understand some of the tribal languages, although others were totally unintelligible to him. Gradually he began to pick up bits of their vocabulary, for he felt a great burden to evangelize these people. He had given up his ambition to become a great leader in the Taway tribe and was now content to serve all the tribes if only he could bring them to Jesus.

Sometimes he visited the refugees by himself. As he counseled them and helped them in practical ways, they sensed that he really cared for them, and many began to listen carefully to his words about Jesus. Eventually several families became Christians.

Finally Peng's sister Noy arrived with her husband Ding and two children, relieved to be reunited with the Taway Christians. She reported that conditions had become very dangerous in Ban Dao and the Mong area. After Noy and Ding settled near the other believers, Ding finally decided to trust in Jesus, but he fell back into his old ways many times.

"I guess I'm like the prodigal son," he told Kathy one day. Several months later Noy reported that Ding had left her and returned to Ban Dao. The pull of the old life had been too much for him.

After his rice was harvested that year, Peng returned to Bible School, realizing he needed more training in order to serve God effectively. One night in Savannakhet he had difficulty getting to sleep, although he was quite tired from a busy day of studying and preaching in the villages outside town. The weather was unusually warm and humid, and there didn't seem to be any air stirring in the crowded dormitory room. Close by he could hear the stray dogs that roamed the streets at night yapping at the full moon. He was relieved when they finally ran off, but then he was distracted by the buzzing noise of mosquitoes trying to get through his sleeping net.

As he tossed and turned on his thin mattress, trying not to awaken the other boys, his thoughts turned to David Fewster who was living alone in the mountains in a village near Kong, carrying on the work there while John and Dorothy Davis were away. Once Peng had stayed there with David for a short time, and they were close friends. David had been present when his mother accepted Christ, and he had also come to Samat's funeral.

Peng turned over on his side, hoping he could relax and doze off, but David was still on his mind. Suddenly he sat up, certain that the young missionary was in serious danger. He felt the Holy Spirit calling him to prayer, and he remembered the missionaries saying that God often gave them special strength and protection in answer to the prayers of their friends. So there under his mosquito net he sat for several hours with his head bowed, asking God to protect his friend David.

The next morning he begged the other students to join him in praying for David's safety. He even convinced the Bible School teachers there was an urgent need, and they canceled some classes so that everyone could intercede for David.

Later they learned what had happened. Because of a sudden threat of communist attack in the area, the local military officials had advised the American Peace Corps fellows living near Kong to leave for a safer place, but no one had said anything to warn David. He had heard distant shooting that night, but the fighting had not come near him. David always felt he had been kept safe from harm at that time because of the prayers of Peng and the other students.

When the semester was over, Peng spent a night in Solane on his way home. Walking through the marketplace the next morning, he saw a familiar face across the street, and realized it was Heng, the leader of the men who had murdered his father! Peng stared at him, unable at first to believe his eyes. Then Heng, who was apparently searching the crowd for someone, looked his way. Recognizing Peng, he smiled grimly and tossed his head arrogantly. A wave of bitterness and fear flooded Peng's consciousness, and he found himself trembling. Quickly Heng turned away and disappeared into the bustling, noisy crowd.

Suddenly Peng realized he was holding his breath and his heart was pounding erratically. Trying to calm himself, he walked home slowly, wild questions surging through his mind. He couldn't help looking over his shoulder several times to see if anyone was following him. Why had Heng come to Solane? To kill him? Where was Lansee?

After he reached the little house he had built near his fields, he considered the matter more calmly and was ashamed. He knew Jesus was able to protect him from any danger that was not in God's perfect plan. Why did he still feel so bitter against Heng? He had tried to forgive him for killing his father, yet he was upset and astounded to see him walking about freely. It didn't seem right that Heng should escape being arrested and punished for his crime.

Peng had tried to leave the matter in God's hands, but never had he thought the guilty one would go free! He knew the authorities in Solane would do nothing, since the murder had taken place in another province, so he wrote the Laotian police in Mong, asking that justice be done.

A few weeks later they replied with the request that he come to Mong immediately so the investigation could be completed, suggesting that perhaps he himself had killed his own father.

Peng realized this was a veiled threat. They probably wanted a bribe, which of course he wouldn't give them, but he was sure he could defend himself and he was anxious that the matter be cleared up. So he packed a few things and went to the airport to get a ride to Mong.

The missionaries were alarmed at the risk he was taking in returning to Mong, for they had heard there was much fighting going on in that area. They begged Peng not to go, but he was determined. He waited at the airport all day, hoping to get a free ride on an army plane. Commercial flights to Mong had long ago ceased, but sometimes civilians were allowed to board the army planes or helicopters going to Mong if there was extra room. There was much activity at the airport that day but no one paid him any attention, and finally the officials told him to go home and forget about ever returning to that part of the country until the war was over.

Later he learned there had been a big battle near Mong at that time, and the entire area had fallen to the Pathet Lao communist forces. The fighting had even reached over to the Taway villages and several had been bombed, leaving many dead and wounded.

Then Peng realized that God had brought the Taway Christians out from the Mong area the previous year in order to deliver them from the fighting that was to come.

His heart ached for his tribe. They were stubborn and unbelieving, yet God loved them. He hoped that their suffering would convince them that the evil spirits couldn't protect them; perhaps even now some of them had turned to the living God. He knew that someday when the war was over he would return and win many of his people to Jesus. And if he truly loved them, he should forgive the ones who had murdered his father, even Heng who was now living near Solane. He asked God to take the bitterness out of his heart, but the pain was still so great that he was unable to go to Heng and witness to him. Loong said he had heard a rumor that Lansee had died of a sudden illness and Heng had left his children with relatives in Ban Dao when he came to Solane.

Occasionally Peng wondered if he shouldn't get married now, for he often felt lonely and in need of a helpmate. He had once been attracted to a girl in the Bible School, but she had shown no interest in him. After all, he was a lowly tribesman with no wealth and little land or security to offer. The fields and wealth of his family had been lost when they had had to flee from their persecutors in Ban Dao. Laotian girls rarely married into tribal families, and he knew of no suitable Christian girls among the tribes near Solane. With his father dead and his other relatives unable to speak much Laotian, he had nobody to arrange a marriage for him according to the usual custom.

Unable to find a solution, he pushed these thoughts to the back of his mind and tried to be content in his Bible study and service for God. If God wanted him to remain single for some reason, he would accept it. He was always willing to minister wherever he was needed, whether it was evangelizing in refugee villages, praying for the sick, preaching in the churches, or just teaching the Christians in their homes. He enjoyed helping teach and supervise the students in the short-term Bible School that the missionaries had recently established in Ban Khat for tribal young people. A six-week course was held once a year, with about fifteen or twenty students coming from various tribes in the area.

Constantly confronted with the tribal people's fear of the spirits and other beings which they believed lived in the fields, streams and mountains,

Peng prayed for special power to do battle with the spirit world. On several occasions he was able to bring deliverance to people who were demon possessed. Understanding how to bind Satan by the name of Jesus and the power of His shed blood, he took the initiative away from the enemy as he proclaimed the Gospel.

There were discouraging times when Peng felt inadequate to handle the problems the people brought to him. Then he would turn to a favorite Scripture that *Than* Ron had often read to him: "We have this treasure in earthen vessels, to show that the transcendent power belongs to God and not to us. We are afflicted in every way, but not crushed; perplexed, but not driven to despair; persecuted, but not forsaken; struck down, but not destroyed." (2 Cor. 4:7-9)

After he graduated from Bible School he returned for a refresher course on several occasions and, observing his gift for preaching and his call to Christian service, one year the Laotian church sent him with three other students to the Phayao Bible Training Center in northern Thailand for further training. The classes at Phayao were not easy, for there everyone spoke Thai instead of Laotian, and all the textbooks were in the Thai language. Peng studied Thai in preparation for this trip, but the lessons were difficult and he had to study very hard.

Even in Thailand, his thoughts often turned to his father's grave back in Ban Dao. He was still greatly disturbed by what had happened. Could his father's death have been prevented? Shouldn't the missionaries have found a place for the Taway Christians to settle near Mong where they could have continued to witness to their tribe?

Often he prayed with tears, asking God to give him peace and take away this hurt and resentment. Then one night the Lord came to him in a vision and quieted his heart with words of comfort. Peng never said much about this experience, but everyone soon noticed that he had found a new peace and strength.

The six months in Thailand passed slowly. Although the teachers and the other students were friendly, the four young people from Laos often felt homesick, and Peng was glad when the semester was finally over. The war in Laos was worsening, and he was anxious to return home.

Soon he was busier than ever, teaching the believers in Ban Khat and evangelizing the refugees who continued to arrive in a steady stream from the hill country northeast of Solane. Feeling lost and confused in their new environment, the displaced tribal people were always glad to see Peng and the missionaries. They eagerly sought their advice about everything including their many illnesses. The most common diseases were malaria, dysentery and worm infestations. Sometimes Peng sent a note with the local bus driver asking the missionaries for help if a case seemed serious, but he knew from personal experience that God could heal. He remembered hearing *Than* John tell how he had been healed of his asthma and hay fever before coming to Laos. So Peng would pray for the sick, and occasionally they would recover before the medicine arrived!

When new church elders were chosen in Solane that year, Peng had the most votes on the first ballot. Appointed to be a minister-at-large, from then on he rotated with the other elders preaching in the Solane church, and also ministered in the tribal villages whenever possible.

A mid-week Bible study had been held in nearby Ban Sip among the Huay people for quite some time, but Peng saw that some of the women and young people needed special teaching. Although they had been Christians for many years, some could not read very well, for in the past education had seemed an unnecessary luxury, especially for girls who would do nothing but rear families and work in the fields with their menfolk. They asked Peng to help them, for now they realized it was important to learn to speak and read Laotian, not only to be able to study the Bible, but also in order to compete with the Lao people and prosper materially.

Peng especially enjoyed teaching the young people, even though they were mostly girls. It was almost like having a family to care for. One girl named Seedaa was unusually bright and quick to learn. Though always full of chatter and fun, she was well behaved and even helped Peng control the class when the students became unruly. When she completed the course and he saw that she had a gift for teaching others, he put her in charge of the women's class.

Hermann Christen often called on Peng for advice in dealing with various problems in the church, and he was always eager to help. Several times a month he would appear at Hermann's door with a big smile, dressed neatly in his usual white shirt and dark trousers, ready to go out and preach with him or just have a quiet visit and a time of prayer.

One day Peng returned home feeling quite ill. Soon he realized he had malaria, but he was not greatly concerned, as he had had it many times before. But then he became extremely weak and feverish and lost track of how long he had been lying on the mat in his house. He was barely conscious when the missionaries finally arrived with medicine and took him home with them. They discovered he had hepatitis as well as malaria. For several weeks he hovered on the edge of death as Christians everywhere prayed for his recovery.

When his fever broke at last, he was quite weak and debilitated. The missionaries felt he needed a high protein diet and plenty of rest, which he was unlikely to get back in his village, so Neville and Joan Peterson invited him to spend a month with them in Ban Jek. Life moved at a slow pace in this small town on the edge of the Mekong River, and Peng spent most of his time alone in prayer and Bible study. In the evenings he would sit on the verandah talking with Neville and Joan as they watched the children play nearby.

He learned that Neville had recently done a study on the distinction between soul and spirit as used in the Bible, listing all the verses where these words were mentioned. Remembering that his father had been deeply interested in this subject, Peng decided to study the verses himself. The missionary's lists were written in English, but Peng was undaunted. He compared the table of contents in Neville's Bible to that in his Laotian Bible and taught himself to recognize the names of the books of the Bible in English, although the English alphabet was unknown to him. Carefully he copied the long list of Bible references that spoke of the soul and those that mentioned the spirit of man. Then he looked up every verse in his own Laotian Bible, studying them thoroughly.

He was thrilled by what he learned, and became convinced that clear teaching on this subject would help tribal people in Laos find deliverance from their many superstitions, especially those relating to the worship of ancestor spirits. He discussed his ideas with Neville and told him how even as a new Christian his father had understood something of the biblical distinction between soul and spirit, and had tried to convey this to the Taway people in the singing debates.

Returning home at last refreshed in body and spirit, Peng plunged back into the work of teaching and evangelizing. His concern for the lost wouldn't allow him to rest or become just a rice farmer. His sisters and his uncle Loong understood his call to Christian work; they looked after his mother whenever he was away, so he could be free to travel wherever he was needed.

21

A Helpmate

THE CHRISTIANS IN Ban Khat felt that Peng was working much too hard. Besides planting and harvesting his rice crops, he was always going off to preach and help people. The church elders decided he needed a wife to help him settle down, so he wouldn't become ill again.

"Peng, come eat dinner with us," elder Chen said after church one Sunday morning.

Peng accepted the invitation gladly, accustomed to having his needs met in this way when traveling from place to place; but he was surprised to discover that the village chief and all the other elders had also been invited.

The rice and *keng* which had been prepared early that morning before church were brought in by Chen's wife and daughter, and everyone ate quickly. Finally the women carried away the empty bowls and rice baskets, and the men began discussing their abundant rice crop.

When there was a pause in their chatter Chen looked at Peng and said firmly, "You need to get married, Peng. Some unbelievers have three wives, but you have none. You work too hard, and you need someone to look after you." The others murmured in agreement, and everyone looked at Peng expectantly.

He smiled and bowed his head respectfully. "Yes, I've known this for quite some time. But I haven't found a suitable Christian girl, and I have no one to negotiate for me."

"We think *Nang* Seedaa from Ban Sip would make you a good wife," the headman said.

Peng's head came up sharply. Surprised, he looked at the men surrounding him. These were his Christian brothers; they wanted him to be happy. He smiled shyly and considered their suggestion. Many of the Huay people in Ban Sip had turned to Buddhism; they even had a temple in their village. But Seedaa came from a good Christian family there. Although much younger than himself, in the past year she had developed into a capable teacher and now had full responsibility for the women's literacy class. She was also attractive and full of fun. Surely she wouldn't be interested in him!

"But would she be willing to marry me?" he asked, aware that he didn't have much to offer.

"She has turned down all other suitors for several years now, but we have observed that she is attracted to you," one elder said. "Anyway, she should be grateful to have someone like you for a husband." Most tribal girls married when they were in their early teens, and Seedaa had puzzled and annoyed her parents by being excessively particular about whom she married.

"I'll pray about it," Peng said.

"We'll approach her parents and find out how much of a dowry they want," Chen offered. "They probably won't require much, as they are quite wealthy, and their main concern is that their daughter have a good Christian husband."

When Peng saw Seedaa at the literacy class later that week, she appeared rather shy and self-conscious. He felt the same way. What did he know about women? One had hurt him badly years ago, and he had found it difficult to understand women ever since, although some of his distrust had been broken down by the friendly girls at Bible School and the gracious attitude of the missionary women. Could this simple tribal girl become a life-partner who would understand his needs and help him in serving the Lord? And could he understand her needs?

His heart sank as he considered the many adjustments they would have to make to become used to each other. Maybe it would be better to remain single.

After class the women left in their usual rush for freedom, followed by the teenagers he taught. Seedaa lingered behind, collecting the books and literacy charts and arranging things on the porch where her class met. When Peng's last student hurried down the steps of the chapel he came outside and found Seedaa still there.

"Have you enjoyed teaching the women, *Nang* Seedaa?" he asked, feeling frustrated that he couldn't think of a better way to start a conversation.

"Yes, very much, but I need some advice on how to help the slow ones." Smilingly she looked up at him, her dark eyes dancing with mirth. She knew he was nervous, but she was determined to become better acquainted. She had admired him for a long time although she realized he had barely noticed her. Now that the church elders had talked to him about her, perhaps he would be more friendly.

Her heart beat wildly, but outwardly she appeared calm. "Some of the women don't believe they could ever learn to read. The lessons are getting difficult and some women are talking of quitting the class. Can you show me how to encourage them?" They sat down on a bench and he gave her some suggestions.

Seedaa really was quite beautiful, Peng thought, admiring her creamy brown skin and her shining black hair pulled back smoothly into a fancy bun that the missionaries must have taught her. It wasn't the usual type of knot that kept falling apart all day, making so many Laotian women look bedraggled and untidy. Little tendrils of hair hung in enticing short curls in front of her dainty ears.

Peng really didn't know what he was saying, but soon they were laughing together at some joke. A warm, happy feeling spread across his chest. It would be fun to live with this young woman!

After that they met for short walks through the woods several times a week, and Peng became more and more attracted to Seedaa. She had a gentle, cheerful temperament that nicely complemented his more serious demeanor and made him feel at ease. He felt peace in his heart as he asked

God for guidance, so he told the elders to proceed with the negotiations.

Seedaa blossomed as Peng courted her, and about a month later the engagement was announced. The missionaries were delighted – they too had been concerned that Peng find a Christian mate.

The wedding was held in Ban Khat because the chapel there was larger. The villagers and missionaries were already seated in the chapel as Peng and Seedaa met the bridesmaid and best man about fifty yards down the road outside so they could approach the building together. Seedaa wore a white blouse and the traditional hand-woven Lao silk skirt in a delicate shade of mauve. She had a pale orchid-colored silk shawl draped gracefully over one shoulder and under the other like an Indian sari, and a garland of bright flowers in her hair. Feeling very serious and self-conscious as he slowly approached the chapel, Peng walked on Seedaa's right. His silk sarong was a light shade of lavender and over his long-sleeved white shirt he wore a shoulder scarf of pure white silk.

Stepping gracefully out of their sandals and leaving them on the porch, the young people went to the front of the crowded chapel and seated themselves on a large mat facing Chen, who was to perform the ceremony. The bride and groom had each been holding a small vase of flowers; they now placed these on the floor before them. At first Peng had sat down with his legs crossed in front of him in casual Taway style, but when Chen frowned at him and whispered a reminder to sit with proper Laotian etiquette, Peng quickly moved his feet to the right, away from Seedaa on his left. She appeared poised and calm, her bare feet hidden modestly by the soft folds of her skirt, but Peng shifted himself several times, feeling nervous and embarrassed, although his feet were decently covered by the pair of new socks he had bought for this occasion.

The missionaries, who had left their shoes on the porch like everyone else, sat on mats on the floor among the Huay and Taway Christians, watching eagerly. Khap and his wife had come a day's journey from their home in Savannakhet. He was dressed smartly in a dark navy blue business suit, white shirt and tie, outshining some of the missionaries. Sitting near her two daughters, Peng's mother Suk looked about at her family proudly, wishing only that Samat were still alive to see his son's happiness.

The ceremony began with a hymn, followed by a Scripture lesson on marriage. Peng and Seedaa exchanged vows and gold wedding rings, and elder Chen pronounced them husband and wife, commending them to God in prayer. Then the two men chosen as witnesses came forward to sign the legal documents of marriage. This was not yet a common practice among tribespeople, but observing that it was done by the Lao Christians, Peng had insisted on it. Presented with a pen, the first man confessed he didn't know how to write, so Chen guided his hand and helped him write a large X in the proper place. The other witness was the village headman. He took his glasses out of his pocket, put them on with great dignity and slowly wrote his name. The district Head Chieftain then signed his name and handed the paper to the bridegroom. Peng wrote his name carefully and then watched Seedaa do the same, proud that she knew how to read and write.

Following the ceremony, a missionary drove bride and groom the short distance to Seedaa's parents' house where they observed the formal tradition of eating their first meal together. Taking a handful of rice and dipping it into salt and roasted hot peppers, Peng and Seedaa ate in unison, signifying that henceforth they would share everything, both the joyful and the sorrowful experiences of life.

After this brief ceremony came the wedding feast! There was much laughter and teasing as the young couple and their guests ate generous helpings of savory chicken *keng*, rice, and a special dessert made from manioc, a root resembling the sweet potato. Tea and water were served instead of liquor, and consequently there was none of the lewd singing and dancing, quarreling and gambling that usually characterized a wedding among unbelievers.

The couple settled down happily to married life. At first they lived with Seedaa's parents, for tradition required the bridegroom to live and work for some time in his in-laws' home. Normally a married couple in Laos didn't move out to be on their own until after their first child was born, and some stayed with their parents indefinitely. However, after a few months Seedaa's father helped Peng build a nice house nearby so he would have more privacy to study and to counsel those who came for spiritual advice. One of the wealthiest men in the village, Seedaa's father was proud of his son-in-law and wanted to help his ministry in every way possible.

The Christians in Ban Sip elected Peng to be an elder in their church, and he was often called to preach, counsel and baptize new believers in other places as well. He tried to stay at home as much as possible, but usually he couldn't refuse when asked to visit the sick or preach in a refugee village that had no pastor. Soon he bought a small motorbike so he could quickly reach the people who lived away from the paved road. If the narrow forest paths were too steep or rocky for the bike, he would walk.

One day a Christian who had been to the market in Solane brought Peng a message that the missionaries needed him. He hurried into town on his motorbike and found Captain Souban, Hermann Christen and several other missionaries and Lao elders gathered in prayer for a young man named Khamta.

Although he had grown up in a Christian home, Khamta had been living a wild life and had not attended church for a long time. Recently he had been ill and had finally come to request prayer, but during the service he had become violent, shouting obscenities. He seemed terrified, out of his right mind, and he refused to go home. For days the missionaries had prayed with him, counseling him and exhorting him to confess the things which weren't right in his life. Since he became violent whenever the name of Jesus was mentioned, they had begun to think he was demon-possessed, but no one had been able to help him. Knowing that Peng had cast out demons on several occasions, the Lao elders had suggested he be called in to help.

As Peng prayed and talked with him, Khamta became more agitated. Finally Peng asked him, "How many demons are in you?"

"Nineteen," Khamta shouted in a guttural voice, flailing his arms wildly.

Peng had learned from his Bible studies and from his father that evil spirits always had names. "What is your name?" he asked, his hand on Khamta's shoulder.

"Thievery," the young man answered in a choking voice totally unlike his normal speech.

"Thievery, I cast you out in the victorious name of Jesus, the Son of God, who died and rose again!"

Khamta jumped up and with an unearthly scream struggled violently against the missionaries who were holding him so he wouldn't harm himself. In spite of the noise and confusion everyone was praying quietly, claiming God's deliverance.

When Khamta finally calmed down, Peng

asked again, "Now, evil spirit, what is *your* name?"

"Lying!" the young man shouted, struggling again.

As the missionaries and elders prayed, Peng cast out each spirit by name until no more answered his challenge. Twenty-nine demons in all came out of Khamta. In his right mind at last, he lay on the floor, exhausted and perspiring.

He seemed fully recovered, but the next morning he quarreled with his father and brother and became quite upset. The church elders and missionaries knew the battle was not over, so they spent the entire day with Khamta in fasting and prayer. Finally he realized he had never been born again but was only a Christian in name. After receiving Jesus as his Savior that day, he had complete deliverance from the oppression of the devil.

When Peng returned home he found Seedaa acting irritable and sulky. "Why were you gone so many days? I needed you," she said.

Chagrined, Peng realized he had forgotten to send a message home explaining his delay. He was used to being single and not having to account to anyone for his whereabouts.

"I'm sorry," he said. "I should have sent a letter or message with someone, but I just didn't think. I couldn't leave until Khamta was well again." He told her it had taken several days to cast out all the demons.

"Why do you always have to get involved? Let the missionaries take care of the problems." She tossed her head in annoyance.

"They said they needed me."

"Well, I needed you too. I didn't feel well enough to teach the literacy class or get firewood because . . . because I'm going to have a baby."

"You're going to have a baby? How wonderful!" Peng smiled broadly and comforted his young wife. He resolved to stay home and be more considerate to her needs.

The baby was born in October 1974, a boy whom Peng promptly called Levi, insisting that he be given a good Bible name. He hoped his son would give himself wholly to God, like the Levites in the Old Testament, and be a minister of God someday.

Peng refused to let Seedaa follow the custom of "sitting by the fire" after the baby's birth. Many people in Laos believed a mother would recover better from childbirth if she would lie beside a fire for two weeks, drinking hot water, to purify her system. This had no pagan religious significance that Peng knew of, but he had learned from the missionaries that it was unnecessary and probably debilitating for women to be subjected to such treatment, especially in hot tropical weather. However, he made sure Seedaa had plenty of rest and good food while regaining her strength.

Peng was very proud of his wife and little son. He had waited many years for a family and was grateful that God had finally answered his prayers.

At first Peng stayed home much of the time with his wife and baby, but soon he was again busy with his pastoral duties. When he was called away overnight Seedaa often went to stay with her parents who lived nearby. Her mother enjoyed helping her care for Levi, but Seedaa was lonely whenever Peng was gone.

She still taught the women's literacy class although often it was difficult to fit it into her busy schedule. She was always up before dawn to pound the husks off the rice that she needed to cook for the day's meals. Then, just to cook a simple *keng* she had either to kill and pluck a chicken or clean a fish, depending on which was available. There was no market in Ban Sip, so she relied upon Peng to buy food whenever he went to Solane, ten kilometers away. Sometimes he forgot to get anything in town, or they didn't have money enough for food. However, the people he ministered to would often show their gratitude by giving him a chicken or a few eggs or maybe just a handful of bamboo sprouts for her to cook in a *keng*.

As the dry season progressed that year such gifts became less than a trickle, and their meals were often little more than rice, eggs, peppers, and salt. Then their few chickens stopped laying eggs.

"We need some better food for Levi," Seedaa told Peng one day. She was breastfeeding her baby, as all women did in Laos, but the infant was slow to gain weight. "Could you get a chicken in town today so I can make him some broth? Then we could also have a chicken *keng*. I'm tired of just rice and peppers." They had only a few laying hens and didn't want to kill one of them.

"We don't have any money," Peng answered. "Remember, I had to use our last bit of cash for bus fare to go up the mountain to visit the Tang family who were so sick last week." His motorbike had been needing repairs for several weeks, but he didn't have the needed parts or any way to transport it down to Solane so a mechanic could fix it.

"If you don't get some meat for us soon, *we'll* all be sick, too," commented Seedaa grimly. "I know you don't want me to ask my parents for help, although they have plenty and would be glad to share with us. Why don't the missionaries pay you for all the work you do? They seem to have plenty of money and food!"

Peng was silent. Seedaa already knew the answer, for they had discussed this many times. The Laotian church sent them money from the evangelistic fund several times a year, acknowledging that Peng was a faithful evangelist among the tribes, but lately that fund had been quite low as all of Laos was suffering from the war and from rising prices in the market place. Other church elders were also feeling the pinch of inflation, even though they were all laymen who raised their own rice. It was difficult to prepare weekly sermons, evangelize the lost, counsel weak Christians, and still do their regular farming, but the Laotian church followed the pattern set by the Brethren missionaries from Switzerland who had first brought the Gospel to Laos. They did not believe church leaders should be a separate class wholly dependent upon others. This did avoid allowing men to become pastors who might secretly desire only the power and apparently easy life of being a leader in the church. However, Peng had to admit there were disadvantages in trying to be an effective pastor and a successful farmer at the same time.

"Our trust is in the Lord, Seedaa, not in the missionaries. They also trust God for the supply of their needs."

Seedaa had no answer to this, for she knew the missionaries did live by faith, and sometimes they even went without things that other foreigners in Laos considered basic necessities. But they always seemed to have enough food!

"Let's pray right now that God will supply our need for meat," Peng suggested, seeing that Seedaa was feeling quite discouraged. They prayed together then and again at bedtime, committing themselves to God and declaring their confidence in Him.

The next morning they were eating their usual meal of rice and hot peppers when Peng's uncle Loong arrived, panting breathlessly from his hurried climb up the mountain. "Let me borrow your rifle, Peng! I saw fresh bear droppings in the forest yesterday, and I think I can track the bear down. I'll give you some of the meat. There will be plenty for all of us!"

Loong came home triumphantly that evening with a bear carcass so large that several men had had to go help him carry it down the mountain. As soon as he heard the news Peng hurried down to Loong's house, lighting his way with a torch of resin and bark chips wrapped tightly in several large leaves.

"What a magnificent bear!" he exclaimed when he saw the animal. "Weren't you afraid when you were tracking it through the forest?"

"Just near the end when the bear saw me and began to charge," Loong admitted with a chuckle. "I climbed a tree real quick and shot it right in the head."

Peng took home his share of the meat and also the bearskin which Loong insisted on giving him. "Since I was using your rifle and bullets you ought to have more than the others, and I know you really need some extra cash, Peng. Maybe you can sell the skin in the Solane market."

Peng wasn't able to sell the bearskin for cash, but he finally traded it for some baby ducks. "When they are grown, we'll have duck eggs to eat," he told Seedaa.

They cared for the tiny ducks carefully and enjoyed watching them grow. "I'm going to give one duck to the Lord as a thanksgiving offering," Peng declared. "God really answered our prayer for meat quickly by helping Loong shoot that bear. I'll sell a duck and give the money to the church."

But he wanted to wait until the ducks were mature, so he could get a good price for the one he sold. "It'll be worth more if it's already laying eggs," he said.

22

The Power of the Word

"I HEAR *THAN* RON'S motorbike coming up the road!" Peng called to Seedaa. They had just finished their noon meal, and he was relaxing on the porch of their home before going back to work in the fields. The harvest season was a busy time, but Peng usually came home at midday to eat with his wife. Then he would hold little Levi and try to keep him quiet so that Seedaa could get some rest.

The spluttering roar of the motorbike grew louder, and a cloud of dust swirled up at the entrance to the village. No one could mistake the sound of Ron's old motorbike, Peng thought, with an inner chuckle.

The bike came to a screeching stop, and suddenly silence once more enveloped the small village. As the dust settled Peng saw that Ron had brought Kathy with him.

"*Sambai baw*! We're here," Ron announced as they dismounted awkwardly, brushing red dust from their hair and clothes, their tired muscles feeling stiff from the long ride.

"*Sambai dee, Than*," Peng responded. "We knew you were coming even before we saw you!" he joked. "That motorbike is certainly noisy, but at least it gets you up the mountain." He handed the baby to Seedaa and nimbly climbed down the ladder from the porch to welcome the missionaries. By then a crowd of friendly neighbors had surrounded Ron and Kathy, asking what the latest news was from Solane. As usual, it was not good.

"We hear that enemy soldiers have taken several more towns on the other side of the mountains," Ron reported. "Every time the North Vietnamese advance in South Vietnam, things get worse here in Laos, too." He shook his head gloomily, and Peng noticed a sad look in his eyes.

"You're not going to have to leave Laos, are you?" he asked in alarm.

"Oh no, not yet anyway. We'll stay as long as we can," Ron assured him. "But that might be only a few more months."

The crowd of neighbors finally dispersed, and Peng invited the missionaries into his house to relax and drink some tea. He knew they drank only boiled water to prevent illness, so he had made a habit of keeping some weak tea brewed and cooled down in a special jar for them. The tea was lukewarm, but Ron and Kathy drank it gratefully.

"How is Levi?" Kathy asked, reaching out her arms to take him from Seedaa. He was almost three months old now but not gaining weight like he should.

"He had diarrhea again yesterday, but he's better today," Seedaa said. Most babies in Laos had frequent stomach upsets, but Levi seemed to be sick much too often.

"I brought a new kind of medicine for him," Kathy said. "If this doesn't help, we'd better take him to the Filipino clinic again and let the doctors there examine him." Life was a constant struggle against disease, especially for children in the villages, and there were very few medical facilities. Kathy had been trained as a nurse and she kept a small supply of medicines with her so she could help those in need.

"How are your children?" Seedaa asked.

"They're fine. A missionary friend is staying with Esther and Danny this afternoon while we're gone," Kathy said. "Stevie and Becky are doing well at school in Malaysia. We had a letter from them just this morning."

"I brought some parts that might get your motorbike going again," Ron told Peng. "Let's go work on it." The bike was quickly repaired, and then the two young couples spent the next hour in Bible study and prayer together. Peng often preached in the village churches, but he himself needed fellowship and encouragement, and Ron and Kathy always felt strengthened spiritually after praying with him.

When they finally had to leave, Peng followed them down the ladder. "I hope you can stay in Laos many more years, but I know it's dangerous for you to be here," he told them. "Aren't you afraid sometimes?"

"Yes . . ." Kathy replied slowly. "Not for myself, because I know God will protect me, but I wonder how I could endure it if I should somehow be separated from Ron or from our children."

"God won't let that happen," Ron assured her, putting his arm around her gently. "We'll just trust the Lord to lead us step by step."

"If you ever do have to leave Laos, don't forget us," Peng said. Bending down and picking up a brown rock from beside the path, he handed it to Ron, saying, "I don't have anything better to give you, but here's a rock you can take with you if you have to go back to America. When you look at it, remember to pray for us."

As the fighting in Laos waxed and waned, the missionaries wondered what the future held. They listened to news broadcasts in English on their shortwave radios every evening to find out what was going on, but Laos was rarely mentioned. There were no reliable sources of news inside the country, only rumors that changed every day. After years of labor under uncertain conditions in this war-torn land, it appeared that the open door in Laos was slowly closing. No one wanted to think of leaving, but they all realized they had to be prepared to evacuate at a moment's notice.

Peng had a very good rice harvest that year. Seedaa often felt too tired to help him in the fields because caring for sickly Levi took a lot of her time and energy. So Peng worked long hours each day.

As he was tying stalks of rice into bundles one day so he could beat them on the ground to thresh them, he began to think of all the nice things he could buy for Seedaa with the money he would get from his abundant crop. He wouldn't need to keep all the rice this year, he thought. He could buy Seedaa a new skirt and blouse, and they could both get some new sandals which they needed badly. Maybe he could also buy a couple of chairs and a small table, or at least some lumber to make them himself. It would be so much easier to study at a table instead of sprawled on the floor. Peng had been around the missionaries long enough to see that some of their "luxuries" were almost necessities.

A canopy of cloudless blue sky stretched above the golden rice fields, but the January air was cool and comfortable. Peng should have been full of energy and happiness, but instead he felt lethargic and despondent. Even though everything was going well for him, he seemed to have lost his joy. He tried to throw off the sense of guilt that was nagging him, but he couldn't. He knew what was wrong, though he had told himself many times it wasn't important.

He had enjoyed eating duck eggs so much that he had delayed trying to sell one of the ducks in town to get his thanksgiving offering for the Lord. He had been justifying himself by the fact that it was harvest time and he was extremely busy. But he knew that didn't justify him before God. Last week all the ducks had suddenly died of a mysterious illness, so now he couldn't keep his promise to the Lord.

Peng knew he had grieved the Spirit of God. Tears began to roll down his cheeks, and he stopped his work and began to pray. "Lord Jesus, forgive me for not keeping my promise. I have been thinking too much about getting things for myself and not enough about you. I do want to put you first in my life from now on." The heavy load seemed to lift from his heart at last, and he knew he was forgiven.

He realized that he had begun to desire material possessions and that this attitude had hindered his effectiveness for God. "Never again will I be so concerned about material things," he said aloud to God. "I will be content to live a simple life so that the Christians I teach will not be stumbled by my bad example."

Looking about him at the golden grain waiting to be harvested, he recalled the many wonderful things God had done for him since he had become a Christian. Finally he said to himself, "I'll sell some of this rice and give the money to God even if I can't buy those other things I wanted."

A few days later, just before the annual church conference, Hermann Christen came to ask Peng to join the missionaries in a day of prayer. Hermann had been deeply depressed since the recent sudden death of his daughter in a tragic accident, and he was also concerned about a number of serious problems in the churches and among the missionaries. The Laotian elders had chosen him to preach at the church conference, but he had felt physically and emotionally unable to do this.

However, the Lord had touched his spirit afresh that week and now he wanted all his colleagues to join him in special prayer that he might be used mightily by God at the conference.

Although Peng hadn't quite finished harvesting his rice, he put his work aside and went to Solane the next morning to meet with the missionaries. All the OMF and Mission Evangelique workers living in Solane set aside the entire day for fasting and prayer, reading the Scriptures together and waiting before the Lord for special words to encourage their brother in Christ. Each of them took a turn praying for Hermann and claiming full victory over Satan.

Before his turn to pray Peng read from Hebrews 12:15 and asked Hermann, "Is there possibly a root of bitterness that is troubling you? Is everything right between you and all the brethren?" It took courage to speak frankly and exhort his dear friend, but Peng had heard there was friction between Hermann and one of the church elders, and he knew that a bad attitude towards others could hinder one's service for God.

"Yes, my conscience is clear," Hermann replied. "I've made things right with Father-of-Danee.[1] I received a nice letter from him last week, and I know we're friends again."

At the end of the day Peng and each of the missionaries prayed, laying hands upon Hermann

---

[1] Sometimes a Lao man is named in this manner after the birth of his first child.

as they gave thanks for victory over Satan and asked that God's blessing would be manifested at the conference.

Peng had only enough money for one round-trip bus fare to the village where the church conference was to be held, but he was determined that Seedaa would go with him. She had missed out on many church activities because of the baby's frequent illnesses. Now that Levi was well again, Peng wanted his wife at his side. "We'll go to the conference together and trust God for the money to get back home," he told her. "God will provide for us."

Although travel passes were difficult to obtain, the meetings were well attended. The Laotian and tribal believers knew that if the missionaries were forced to leave Laos soon, they would have to carry on by themselves, and they wanted to prepare themselves for the trials that might be ahead.

Unaware of Peng's need, a missionary spoke to him privately soon after the conference began. "God told me to give this to you," he said, handing Peng some money which proved to be more than sufficient for their bus fare home. When an opportunity was given for testimonies in one of the meetings that week, Peng was the first to stand, eager to share this answer to prayer.

That gift also made it possible for Peng and Seedaa to go to Savannakhet in April that year to teach at the Youth Camp, and Peng also attended the Elders' Conference which was held a few days later. He enjoyed the teaching given by Eli, Meekay and Souban on leadership. Besides the elected leaders from the 21 organized assemblies of southern Laos, several potential leaders also came to the conference from some of the twenty or thirty emerging churches. Each assembly was independent and free to run its own affairs.

Peng and Seedaa stayed on after the Elders' Conference for a month-long extra session of the Bible School, which was held in Savannakhet for advanced students, part of the fourth year of study. Nine students were enrolled. The elders in charge felt that Peng had much valuable experience to share and asked him to teach two lessons a week on "Visiting and Counseling Christians."

Suddenly rioting erupted in Savannakhet and other major towns as young people attending the government schools protested against the presence of foreigners in Laos. Inflamed by news of the collapse of South Vietnam and Cambodia, the students were very agitated, and it was dangerous for anyone to be out on the streets. Peng heard that even more serious rioting was occurring in Solane, and he was glad that Seedaa and the baby were still with him, staying with Khap and his family on the edge of town. As soon as the classes were over Peng and his family returned to Ban Sip, relieved to be away from the unrest in the city.

Although the students had not been demon-strating specifically against them, the missionaries felt uneasy. They were aware that their presence was becoming more of an embarrassment and danger to the believers than a help. One day after a missionary had visited a Laotian Christian in his home, a government official immediately came to interrogate him on what the foreigner had said.

So it was that, after eighteen years in southern Laos, the OMF had to withdraw its workers. In the final days they were able to take nearly all their personal possessions across the river into Thailand, and also some of the mission property. This involved getting permission from the new authorities and passing checks by police, customs and a communist soldier.

Just before the last missionaries left, a large shipment of Bibles and New Testaments arrived and was allowed to enter the country. Everyone rejoiced at this evidence that God was still in control and would watch over the church in Laos during the dark days ahead.

The new government allowed the Christians to meet for worship on Sunday mornings, but no other meetings were allowed, nor could they pass out tracts to unbelievers. The Bible School in Savannakhet was closed and the property confiscated. Although some nominal Christians may have denied Christ when pressured by the authorities, most of the believers remained firm, some through severe testing. They attended the compulsory political re-education classes but clung stubbornly to their faith in Jesus.

Living conditions became very difficult for everyone. The markets closed up, and the economy fell apart. It was almost impossible to survive unless a person had his own source of food.

One of Peng's best friends among the Christians in Solane was a soldier named Stephen. About the same age as Peng, Stephen had served in the Laotian army all his adult life, and for many years his wife and children had lived in the army camp with him. When the new government took over, the army was disbanded and life in the camp was worse than in a slum. The men there had no paddy fields for growing rice, and the ground around their huts was unsuitable for gardens. Sometimes Stephen rode his bicycle up to Ban Khat to visit with Peng and the other Christians. Peng and Seedaa enjoyed his fellowship and often gave him food to take home. Having a garden and several rice fields, Peng was faring much better than people in town, so he invited Stephen to bring his wife and five children to live near him in Ban Khat.

Stephen didn't want to become a burden on his friends or draw the attention of the new government to them, so he declined this generous offer. But he began taking his family out to visit Peng on the weekends. The good meals and the rich fellowship with the Christians in Ban Khat made the ten-kilometer walk seem quite insignificant! Weary of the struggle for survival in Solane, Cantoe and the children looked forward to these excursions with Stephen.

When they arrived in Ban Sip one Saturday morning, Stephen and Cantoe found Peng sitting on his verandah looking very dejected. He didn't get up to welcome them but motioned to them to come up the ladder. The excited chatter of Stephen's children subsided suddenly when they noticed that Peng's eyes were filled with tears. They looked uncertainly at their parents, wondering what had happened.

"What's wrong?" Stephen asked, kneeling beside his friend. Peng tried to speak but made only a choked sound as his tears overflowed.

"Seedaa? Are you all right?" Cantoe looked through the doorway into the house. "Oh no!" she gasped. "What happened to Levi?"

The child's cold, still body was lying on the wooden floor, wrapped in a blanket. Seedaa sat nearby, her bowed face covered with her hands, her body heaving with sobs of grief.

Eventually Peng was able to tell them, in a choked voice with many tears, that Levi had died in the night. "He was sick yesterday, but it didn't seem more serious than other times. He became very feverish in the evening and cried a long time before he fell asleep. There was no way we could get him to Solane or to the Filipino clinic in the night, and we hoped he was getting better. But he died in his sleep early this morning."

The child was buried after a brief memorial service that afternoon. Cantoe took over the household duties so Seedaa could rest. Her tears had finally abated and now she sat listlessly staring into the distance, unable to sleep and unwilling to talk. Her only child had died! What was there to live for? They had tried to serve God faithfully, and yet He had allowed this terrible thing to happen.

Cantoe had never lost a child, yet she had been through other trials and disappointments, and she sensed the bitter questions that were flooding Seedaa's mind. She sat down near her and began to talk quietly.

"My grandmother once told me that every trial is sent to us for a purpose. She lost her husband when she was just a young woman with only one child. Her husband, my grandfather, died while on a trip to sell some cattle in Vietnam. She loved him very much and refused to marry again. They had just recently become Christians, and all the other young men she knew were unbelievers. She knew it would be wrong to marry a non-Christian, so she managed to raise my mother all by herself, though it was very difficult."

Seedaa made no comment but she looked expectantly at her friend, her interest aroused. Hoping to help her forget her grief for a while, Cantoe went on with the story.

"When my mother was a teenager she was very popular and was considered to be quite beautiful, and many young men tried to court her. She wouldn't even listen to them, because they weren't Christians. She was sure God would eventually send a nice Christian young man to marry her, but there weren't many who believed in Jesus in those days. Finally her mother suggested that she marry a widower who had four children. He was a Lao evangelist who traveled all over Laos preaching to the tribes as well as to the Laotians, and after his first wife died he needed a Christian woman to raise his children.

"My mother was afraid at first to take on such heavy responsibilities, for she was barely twenty years old, and she wasn't even sure she loved the man although she admired him greatly. But then she got acquainted with him and he asked her to marry him. They had a wonderful life serving God together. Sometimes she traveled with him and helped teach the women in the villages. Eventually she had children of her own, including myself, and then my father died suddenly in a cholera epidemic, leaving her with a large family to raise."

Seedaa's eyes were now fixed on Cantoe, and her tears had dried. She was beginning to realize that others had suffered much greater losses than she had.

"Life hasn't been easy for my mother," Cantoe continued, "but I've never heard her complain. She says God always keeps His promises and never allows us to be tested more than we can bear. You've lost your precious little Levi, and I know your heart will always ache to have him back, but at least you still have Peng, and you can have other children someday."

Cantoe put her arms around her friend as Seedaa began to sob again. "It's all right to cry," she told her. "God understands how you feel, for His Son died, too. Now you know how hard it was for God to let Jesus come die for us."

Stephen and Peng also talked and cried and prayed together a great deal that weekend. Peng couldn't understand God's purpose in taking Levi from them, but as he spent much of the following week reading his Bible he found many verses that comforted and strengthened him. He was soon busy teaching in the villages again, and this helped him forget his grief and heartache.

It was harder for Seedaa, left at home in the empty house. She was unnaturally quiet and subdued for several months. She did her work mechanically, never speaking more than necessary, never smiling. All the light seemed to have gone out of her face. Peng tried to draw her out and comfort her, but she withdrew from him. For several months she continually sought excuses to keep from attending church. But when she realized she was going to have another child in the spring, her attitude began to change. Finally one Sunday before church she asked the elders to pray for her that she might come back into full fellowship with the Lord.

"I'm sorry for my bitter spirit, and I want to serve the Lord again," she said.

Gradually Stephen and Cantoe's visits became less frequent, as the government increased their surveillance of the Christians. One Saturday Peng went to buy some sandals in Solane. There was no food for sale in the market these days, and he was shocked at the rising prices in the few shops that were still open. He stopped to visit Stephen and

Cantoe on his way home, for he hadn't seen them for several months. They read God's Word and prayed together, encouraging one another in the Lord.

As Peng was preparing to leave, Stephen took him aside and whispered to him, "I've decided I must get my family out of Laos as soon as possible. The government is threatening to take children away from Christian parents, to educate them in communist doctrines. I want my children to have a good education and not have to study the communist propaganda."

"I understand how you feel," Peng said softly.

"We'll be leaving quite soon," Stephen went on. "I've applied for a travel pass to Savannakhet. My wife wants to visit her mother there. And then . . . perhaps God will provide a way for us to . . ."

There was no need to say the words. Peng knew what he meant. "It's very dangerous to try to escape across the Mekong River," he whispered.

"I know," Stephen answered. "But it's more dangerous for my family to stay in Laos, for already our children are being forced to attend some propaganda classes. You are the only one I have told. Pray that we'll reach Thailand safely."

Peng never saw Stephen and Cantoe again, but many months later a friend whispered to him that they had arrived safely in Thailand and were expecting to go on to America as soon as they could find sponsors.

The government paid little attention to the simple tribespeople living in the mountains, for they had plenty else to do trying to improve the economy and re-educate the Laotians in the lowland towns and villages. So Peng was able to quietly continue teaching the Christians in the villages around Ban Khat, and sometimes on Sunday mornings he even preached in the chapel in Solane, for the Laotian believers also needed encouragement.

One Sunday he recognized his friend Meekay in the congregation. After the service they talked eagerly, recalling their Bible School days and the many times they had traveled together preaching in the villages before the missionaries left.

"When are you going to get married, Meekay?" Peng asked.

"Life is too uncertain to think of such things now," Meekay said soberly. "How is your family? I heard your son died last year." Meekay had been living with his parents near Savannakhet and hadn't been to Solane to see Peng for many months.

"Yes, God took Levi home to heaven. It's hard to understand why he wasn't healed, but God has drawn us closer to Himself through this sorrow. We have another son now, and Seedaa is more interested in serving the Lord than she used to be. Do you hear any news from the missionaries?"

Meekay shook his head. "No, it's dangerous for anyone to receive letters from outside the country, so that's probably why they don't write."

"I miss them very much. I wonder if Stephen and Cantoe are in America now," Peng said quietly, dropping his voice and looking around. Even among Christians a person had to be careful what he said.

The two young men walked down the street a short way, chatting together. When they were a safe distance from others, Meekay said softly, "I heard that Stephen and his family are still in the refugee camp in Thailand. Someday I'm going to try to escape across the river, too. I feel I could serve the Lord better where there is freedom. Maybe I could help make tapes for the Christian radio programs that are broadcast into Laos." In the past Meekay had often helped the missionaries with this work.

Peng nodded understandingly. Meekay had studied the Bible in Switzerland for three years and he could speak French and even some English.

"Yes, you could help the refugees adjust to life outside of Laos," he agreed. "You know what it's like to live in a western country." They had heard rumors that many countries were accepting refugees from the large camps in Thailand that were overflowing with people who had escaped from Laos and Cambodia.

"My place is to stay here," Peng said firmly. "It would be too hard to get my family out of Laos, for tribespeople traveling near the border would attract a lot of attention. Anyway, I wouldn't want to live outside Laos even though I do long to have freedom. I wouldn't be of much use to anyone in America or Switzerland, and someday I must return to my father's village on the other side of the mountains. The Taway people there need to hear of Jesus."

Several months later Peng heard that Meekay had successfully escaped across the river near Savannakhet. He thought about the news all day as he plowed his paddy fields. That evening he sat alone on the verandah until late, his family already asleep. The cicadas and tree frogs filled the dark forest around him with unrelenting noise, but he didn't hear them.

In his mind he heard the voices of his friends – John and Dorothy Davis who had led him to the Savior, the women who had taught him in Mong, his teachers at Bible School. He remembered Ron and Kathy Smith exhorting him to stand true to Jesus no matter what the cost. He recalled many happy church meetings with the missionaries from Switzerland. All these friends were gone now, even Meekay and Stephen.

Peng sighed, and tears welled up in his eyes. As they spilled down his brown face, he looked up at the star-filled sky. Then he remembered that these friends who had brought so much happiness into his life could see some of the same stars on the other side of the world. Suddenly he sensed their love reaching out to him and their prayers upholding him.

He would be strong. He had to be strong, because his people needed him. There were many who had not yet heard the name of Jesus.

He looked up again at the silvery moon and

the bright stars. Because of their persistent radiant witness, he had searched for the Creator and found Him. He was not alone, for God was still in Laos. The stars above and the fragrant forest about him were witness to His unfailing care.

Relying on Jesus, the Great Spirit who had created all things and who made the rock flowers bloom, Peng knew he would find strength to stand firm for the Word of God, no matter what trials lay ahead.

Epilogue

THE CHURCH IN Laos has continued to function in spite of government restrictions. Christians are not allowed to share the Gospel openly or pass out tracts, but they are permitted to celebrate Christmas and meet for worship on Sunday mornings.

Although some may have denied Christ, others have stood firm under severe pressures, and there have even been many new converts. A Swiss Christian who was in Laos recently was able to meet with many of the Laotian believers. His reports indicate that the church is stronger and more healthy than ever before. In one village in southern Laos a larger chapel has been built to accommodate the increase in believers. A group of tribal converts has been reported near the Vietnam border, possibly the result of village evangelism done there when the OMF first went into the country.

Armand Heiniger, who visited Laos in early 1982, was allowed to meet with the believers and share in their church services. He said that Savannakhet appeared quite run-down, dirty and depopulated, so many merchants having departed. By contrast the roads were in good order and the chapel was well kept up, with an attractive courtyard full of bright tropical flowers.

He was told that about fifteen thousand Christians had been registered by the government, representing nearly a hundred groups meeting across the country for regular worship. Probably less than half of these are functioning as fully organized churches. Accurate statistics are very difficult to obtain, and others estimate there are only about three thousand Christians in Laos, a small amount in a population of three million – but response to the Gospel has always been slow in a Buddhist culture.

The Hmong tribe in northern Laos was unusually responsive to the Gospel in past years. These people have been a special target of the new government, and their number has dwindled significantly as thousands have fled to Thailand for refuge. Very few Laotian Christians have escaped from the southern provinces and none of the tribal people, as far as we know.

Souban is now pastor of a Laotian church near New Orleans, Louisiana. Married to a Christian girl he met in the refugee camp, Meekay lives in California where he prepares the radio programs that the Far Eastern Broadcasting Company beams into Laos on medium wave from their transmitter in the Philippines. For years the Laotian programs were broadcast only on short wave, but now every radio set in Laos should be able to receive the Gospel message.

Stephen and his family live in the northwestern part of the United States, where in his spare time he assists new refugees from Laos as they struggle to adapt to the fast pace of life in the western world.

We have had no direct news from Peng, but hear he is still busy teaching the Christians and winning souls to Jesus.

An Asian brother recently brought out this message from the Christians in Laos: "We are learning to depend on the Lord in a greater way, independent of outside financial help. This is a real source of joy for us." Considering that there is often a severe shortage of food and medicine, this statement reveals a growing maturity in Christ.

The Savannakhet Bible School has not been reopened, but as far as we know the teachers continue to minister quietly in their home villages. Although Laos has apparently been spared the excesses of political power which caused thousands to be murdered elsewhere in southeast Asia, it cannot be easy for the Christians to live under a totalitarian government. Certainly they must face daily testings and pressures more severe than any we can imagine.

The spiritual battle for souls in Laos is not over. Taking up the invincible weapons of faith and prayer, Christians everywhere must join in spiritual warfare for this needy and almost-forgotten land. Our Laotian brothers and sisters desperately need our intercession, that the powers of darkness may be restrained and they may be able to share Jesus with the many tribes who have not yet heard the good news of salvation.

Peng and his brethren are counting on our prayers. Let us not fail them!